ON-THE-LEVEL

PATRICIA McLAGAN   PETER KREMBS

**PERFORMANCE
COMMUNICATION
THAT WORKS**
NEW EDITION

Berrett-Koehler Publishers
San Francisco

Berrett-Koehler Publishers, Inc.
155 Montgomery Street
San Francisco, CA 94104-4109
Tel: (415) 288-0260   Fax: (415) 362-2512

ORDERING INFORMATION

Individual sales. Berrett-Koehler publications are available through most
bookstores. They can also be ordered direct from Berrett-Koehler at the
address above.

Quantity sales. Special discounts are available on quantity purchases by
corporations, associations, and others. For details, contact the "Special Sales
Department" at the Berrett-Koehler address above.

Orders for college textbook/course adoption use. Please contact Berrett-
Koehler Publishers at the address above.

Orders by U.S. trade bookstores and wholesalers. Please contact Publishers Group West, 4065 Hollis Street, Box 8843, Emeryville, CA 94662. Tel: (510)
658-3453; 1-800-788-3123; Fax: (510) 658-1834.

Printed in the United States of America

Printed on acid-free and recycled paper that is composed of
85% recovered fiber, including 15% post-consumer waste.

Library of Congress Cataloging-in-Publication Data
McLagan, Patricia A.
　　On-the-level : performance communication that works / Patricia
McLagan, Peter Krembs. — New ed.
　　　　p.　　cm.
　　Includes index.
　　ISBN 1-881052-76-1 (alk. paper)
　　　1. Communication in personnel management.　2. Employees—Rating
of.　I. Krembs, Peter.　II. Title.
HF5549.5.C6M33　　　1995
　　658.4'5—dc20　　　　　　　　　　　　　　　　　　95-18624
　　　　　　　　　　　　　　　　　　　　　　　　　　　　　CIP

CONTENTS

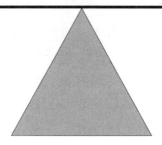

PREFACE   vii

INTRODUCTION   New Issues, New Players, New Power   1

The New Era of Communication   2

Assumptions About Performance
Communication   3

Communicating On-The-Level   7

What You Can Expect   7

A Final Note Before You Go On   9

PART I   Hallmarks of On-The-Level Communication   11

CHAPTER 1   What Is On-The-Level Communication?   13

Performance Communication and
Organizational Culture   14

Guiding Principles of
On-The-Level Communication   15

Person-to-Person Performance
Communication   19

Where Do You Stand?   20

Key Points   23

CHAPTER 2   The On-The-Level Process:
Six Communication Skills   25

On-The-Level Communication Skills   26

Receptive Skills   28

Expressive Skills   33

Staying Alert to Skill Outcomes   39

Communication Games   40

Keeping the Human Element   46

Where Do You Stand?   47

Key Points   50

CHAPTER 3   Being an Observing Participant   51

Recognizing the Power of the Observing
Participant   52

The "STOP" and "SEE" Model   54

Practice, Practice, Practice   61

Where Do You Stand?   62

Key Points   65

PART II   On-The-Level Communication at Work   67

CHAPTER 4   Getting Goal Agreement   69

Common Problems   70

Guidelines for Successful Communication   73

Where Do You Stand?   91

Key Points   94

CHAPTER 5   Giving and Receiving Feedback   95

Common Problems   96

Guidelines for Successful Communication   98

Where Do You Stand?   116

Key Points   118

CHAPTER 6   Delivering and Digesting
Tough Messages   119

Common Problems   120

Guidelines for Successful Communication   124

Where Do You Stand?   137

Key Points   140

CHAPTER 7   Discussing Learning and Development   141

Common Problems   142

Guidelines for Successful
Communication   144

Where Do You Stand?   160

Key Points   162

CONCLUSION   163

INDEX   169

ABOUT THE AUTHORS   179

PREFACE

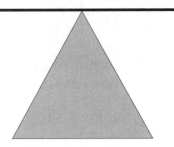

The basic premise of this book is that On-The-Level (OTL) communication—characterized by directness, respect, shared responsibility, and purpose—is an essential ingredient for business success in today's Information Age. Contemporary businesses require informed participation throughout the organization, from top to bottom. In contrast, businesses operating in the Industrial Age confined decision making to the executive ranks. In our view, this practice no longer provides a competitive advantage. Instead, responsible and informed participation—made possible through OTL communication at all levels of the organization—is necessary for success in today's rapidly changing business environment.

This book focuses on using OTL communication in workplace discussions about performance and development; however, it has applications beyond these issues. Whenever the output of work must be greater than the contribution of a single individual—that is, when teamwork, innovation, trust, and quick response are required—individuals must be able to communicate On-The-Level.

▲ How to Use This Book

On-The-Level is a book for anyone who needs to plan, execute, or participate in more effective and less fearful face-to-face communication about work and work performance. This includes a diverse group: managers, individual contributors, team members and leaders, customers, suppliers, and colleagues.

On-The-Level is divided into two parts. Part I, "Hallmarks of On-The-Level Communication," contains Chapters 1 through 3 and gives a detailed explanation of the OTL Guiding Principles and Communication Skills, the communication games that people play, and the process of being an Observing Participant. Part II, "On-The-Level Communication at Work," covers applications of OTL principles and skills in specific work-related situations: goal agreement (Chapter 4), feedback (Chapter 5), tough messages (Chapter 6), and learning and development (Chapter 7).

▲ Changing the Way You Communicate

On-The-Level is designed for interactive learning. It provides many opportunities for you to pause and think about how the issues and actions discussed relate to you and how you can use the guidelines and skills presented to improve your performance communication.

Each chapter begins with a story about a communication situation. These and other scenarios throughout the text have been derived from real situations encountered by real clients. Additional examples of situations and difficulties are given in the "Common Problems" sections in Chapters 4 through 7.

As you read, remember that *thought* (or knowing) is different from *action*. In order to really change and improve your communication habits, you must commit to trying new behaviors and challenging old beliefs that may inhibit your development. Each chapter in Part II provides a series of specific, realistic suggestions for taking action in a section called "Guidelines for Successful Communication."

Following the discussion in each chapter, review the questions in "Where Do You Stand?" Use them to help determine your strengths and weaknesses and to commit to those actions that will be most helpful for improving your performance communication.

This is a practical guide. You can absorb the information in many ways. Skim it. Scan it. Read parts of it or all of it. The "Key Points" section at the end of each chapter provides a quick overview of the content. Use this book as a reference any time you prepare for a performance discussion. It will provide guidance, moral support, ideas for improvement, or a perspective on the situation that will increase your effectiveness.

▲ On-The-Level Workshops

In addition to this book, McLagan Learning Systems, Inc., has developed a powerful, one-day workshop, On-The-Level: Communicating About Performance. Included in this experience is an opportunity for you to get feedback from others on your On-The-Level communication practices and to practice new skills and behaviors in a safe, learning-focused environment.

Use the card included in the back of this book to get more information about the course and its availability in your area. If, for some reason, you don't have a card or have additional questions, comments, or suggestions about the book or the workshop, please contact:

McLagan Learning Systems, Inc.
715 Florida Avenue South
Golden Valley, MN 55426
Telephone: 1-800-878-2034

We encourage and welcome your feedback and inquiries.

Patricia McLagan
Peter Krembs

INTRODUCTION

New Issues, New Players, New Power

This quarter, Carl's the leader of a cross-functional quality improvement team working on a new budgeting process for the company. It's been a difficult project throughout, in part, because the team has had to satisfy many internal customers and external suppliers. They've done a good job of listening to a lot of customers and suppliers, hearing about their issues and ideas.

Now that the first draft of the new budgeting process is ready, Carl plans to meet individually with a few customers to discuss what's been proposed and why. He's nervous, though. He thinks that a couple of the people he has to meet with will want features that the team doesn't feel it can provide. Carl wants to reach agreement among everyone involved and is willing to look at all feasible alternatives. But he feels that the

proposal the team has come up with reflects the best overall interests of all key groups. In his one-on-one meetings with customers, Carl wants to gain real support for the plan. He's not confident, though, that he can make this happen, especially in meeting with some of the senior managers.

Carl faces a difficult communication situation, and he doesn't feel prepared to deal with it. What should he do?

▲ The New Era of Communication

Everyone communicates. The question is: With how much success? Many people feel unprepared for the intense communication challenges they face every day. Some take courses or read about face-to-face communication, hoping to improve these skills. Communication is certainly a common and ongoing topic.

Rapidly occurring changes in the nature of work and the workplace itself have made the need for effective communication even more important. Work today is more complex, requiring greater teamwork. Collaboration such as this demands flexibility, learning, and shared vision. Person-to-person communication plays a key role in all these areas.

The workplace has also changed. Most people prepared for a workplace that was hierarchical, relatively stable, proceduralized, and driven by internal standards. But globalization, accelerated competition, customers' demands for quality, and a tougher economic environment have changed all that. People today need to talk with each other across levels and boundaries to keep information moving, to make decisions, to set and reset priorities, and to ensure quality and creativity.

It follows that with changes to work and the workplace, responsibilities for communication have changed, too. In the past, communication was a key managerial responsibility, and accountability for it increased with level and position. Managers communicated plans and strategies; they told (or were supposed to tell) staff members what their jobs were. But while managers coached, supervised, disciplined, recognized, and reviewed performance, staff members' roles in communication were pretty much ignored. Staff were supposed to listen and follow orders. Another problem was the limited amount of communication between customers and suppliers. Even when it occurred, much communication at this level was "win-lose" in nature.

Today, responsibility for communication needs to be shared. If there's something to say, it must be said—respectfully and truthfully—in order to get results and relationships that work. Power differences are no longer reasons for avoiding direct communication. Both parties should be respected and involved, listening and talking, challenging and creating.

In the contemporary workplace, inadequate communication has many bad consequences. For instance, if people don't communicate, they can't be aligned, which wastes resources and leads to working at cross-purposes. If people aren't told how well they're doing or are unable to learn quickly from mistakes and successes, productivity suffers. Without effective communication, good ideas don't come to the fore, problems don't get immediate attention, and decision making doesn't consider important information. Poor communication prevents development of a competitive advantage and erodes the advantage where it exists. In addition, poor communication takes away people's energy, individually and collectively. As a result, they spend time guessing, defending, protecting, and strategizing about how to win.

Person-to-person communication is the "oil" that makes all parts of an organization work together without destructive friction. And as with an engine, the "oil level" has to be regularly checked and maintained. To do so requires ongoing learning and improvement of everyone's ability to interact respectfully, directly, and with shared responsibility for success.

▲ Assumptions About Performance Communication

Communication is by nature a complex topic, but it's especially complicated when it focuses on performance. This is true in part because performance is a matter of self-esteem for most people. We put our ideas, our energy, and even some of our life's purpose into what we do. So talking about performance issues such as goals, roles, feedback, and development can stir up a surprising amount of emotion.

Communication would be simpler and easier if we could provide step-by-step instructions about how to do it successfully. But the fact is, no set of pat procedures or techniques exists. Communication is ongoing and interactive, specific to a given situation and the people in it. Even the most skilled communicator may look back on an exchange and say, "I could've done it differently." And of course, no one can or should control the reactions and behaviors of other people in discussions.

What you *can* control is how *you* approach communication. Consider these observations about effective communication and how they apply to you as a communication giver and receiver:

- Communication among people in an organization is ongoing, whether we realize it or not. We all receive and deliver messages about performance: goals, careers, priorities, problems, and development. Unless we give it deliberate attention, performance communication is often incomplete and indirect.

- When we don't receive information directly, we rely on our own interpretations of nonverbal or ambiguous messages. These interpretations are likely to be loaded with suspicion, negativity, and distrust when communication is deliberately indirect and even secretive.

- Communication is central to an organization's success, which makes it a potential battleground for power and control. In organizations that care about quality and innovation (particularly in an information and service economy), we must avoid this battle; power and control must be spread throughout. We—people—are the most valuable resource in any organization. When we want to know or say something, it's critical that we be able to speak directly. Withholding information or taking a superior stance in interpersonal communication is an abuse of power that organizations can no longer afford.

- Effective person-to-person communication makes good personal as well as business sense. When information is "on the table," we can solve problems and make choices about future work or development with confidence. Certainly, we may find some information and feedback hard to deal with, but tough messages can't be avoided. Nothing drains energy and trust from an organization like telling half-truths and avoiding unpleasant information. Direct communication is a right and a responsibility that we should all share, no matter what our role or position.

- Communication can't be direct unless both parties involved play active roles in making it happen. Performance communication is a shared responsibility. This means that all of us—managers and staff members, customers and suppliers, team leaders and team members—need to be fully aware of how to communicate successfully. Players in all roles have to develop strong communication skills and use them deliberately and responsibly. We must each own the results of the interaction.

- *Judgment* and *subjectivity* are basic features of organizational life and thus unavoidable features of communication. We rarely find situations in which the facts are clear and the so-called right options obvious. For effective communication to occur, both parties have to be willing and able to express judgments and opinions based on incomplete and sometimes contradictory information. We also need to become aware of our personal biases and acknowledge their effects on judgments and opinions.

- Ideally, all performance communication would be objective and neutral, but the truth is, emotional and psychological factors almost always enter in. It may sound good to "separate people from performance," but performance is a personal matter. Issues of self-esteem, power and relationships, and personal commitments and desires are often imbedded in performance. A call for change may also stir up personal issues; some natural defensiveness or grieving may occur when we're asked or otherwise prompted to do something different. Since communication is and will continue to be a human process, we must both accept that personal issues are part of it and channel the emotion and energy that naturally result toward constructive goals. Denying personal and even irrational factors is a sure way to derail effective person-to-person interactions.

- We need to distinguish between *intentional* and *random* communication. Generally, performance communication should be intentional; that is, it should support a purpose. To do so consistently requires high levels of thought, awareness, self-insight, and planning. But we need to keep in mind that *intentional* does not mean *inflexible*. A conversation that might start out with the purpose of solving one problem might intentionally evolve to clarify another. Since person-to-person communication is a shared responsibility, we, as individuals, can never control its outcome.

- Effective performance discussions can't be mechanical or form driven; rather, they require judgment and flexibility by both participants. It's important to acknowledge that each of us brings different communication skills and perspectives to a conversation. No form, policy, or procedure can ensure effective person-to-person communication. And none of these devices or plans can interfere with effective communication if everyone understands and is committed to making it happen. Forms, guides, and other tools may be handy means of achieving results, but they should never become ends in themselves.

Effective performance communication is an interesting challenge. To meet it, we have to reach new levels of *awareness, responsibility,* and even *risk*. Each party in a communication exchange contributes to its success or failure. We're each responsible for how we use power and information. And we each need to move beyond personal fears and emotional barriers to construct (or reconstruct) our own relationships and the very culture of the organization itself.

▲ Communicating On-The-Level

By understanding what effective communication is and by developing the skills to put that knowledge to work, you can improve the quality of your communication. The On-The-Level (OTL) communication approach outlined in this book will give you the knowledge and skills needed to make that improvement.

OTL communication is intentional, not random. It characterizes discussions in the workplace that are open and direct, respectful and responsible, deliberate and focused on output. Individuals communicate On-The-Level when they commit to and take responsibility for understanding each other and working out problems together. In order to do so, they need to have the communication skills necessary to hold purposeful discussions.

On-The-Level communication is not a solo performance; it's the responsibility of both parties in an exchange. If both parties honestly assess how well they communicate now and thoughtfully apply the proven communication skills and guidelines presented in this book, they'll make strides in setting goals, assessing performance, resolving problems, and planning for future work and development.

Before you go on to the rest of this book, think about the complexity or difficulty of being On-The-Level in your work situation: getting goal and role agreement, renegotiating priorities, giving and receiving feedback, supporting development. Respect and appreciate that you *won't* be able to proceduralize your interactions. This mindset will serve as an important base for your continuous improvement in person-to-person communication.

▲ What You Can Expect

The On-The-Level approach is rooted in the notion that effective person-to-person communication is a cornerstone of excellent performance and a good work climate. OTL communication is also a key to deep personal satisfaction and success in today's very complex, changing, and often crazy work environment. Communicating On-

The-Level is important in every human interaction, every day, including informal and personal discussions. However, in this book, we focus on those discussions between people that enable them to work together for performance success. Specifically, we focus on:

Hallmarks of On-The-Level Communication

- *What Is On-The-Level Communication?*—Chapter 1 presents the Guiding Principles that underlie the OTL approach.

- *The On-The-Level Process: Six Communication Skills*—Chapter 2 discusses six communication skills in terms of key behaviors, intended outcomes, and practice guidelines and also examines communication games played by both receivers and senders.

- *Being an Observing Participant*—Chapter 3 looks at the importance of being both inside and outside your performance conversations, exploring the roles of consciousness, purpose, awareness, and mindset in communication success.

On-The-Level Communication at Work

- *Getting Goal Agreement*—Chapter 4 presents goals as agreements among key stakeholders and emphasizes how reaching such agreements is an ongoing process.

- *Giving and Receiving Feedback*—Chapter 5 defines *feedback* as both a process and product of communication, in which information is exchanged for the purpose of evaluation or correction; again, the ongoing nature of such communication is stressed.

- *Delivering and Digesting Tough Messages*—Chapter 6 considers one of the most difficult communication challenges: giving and receiving unpleasant information; guidelines are given for preparing for the situation and focusing on the problem, which can help lessen the emotional impact of the message.

- *Discussing Learning and Development*—Chapter 7 stresses the importance of individual learning and development, particularly in this era of continual change, and discusses the role of communication in both planned and experiential learning.

This book is for everyone, no matter what your level of communication skill and knowledge. If you're shy and lack confidence in your communication skills, OTL will help you begin to have some successes. And if you're skilled and confident, OTL will provide some new perspectives, chances for reflection, and specific tools to add to your capabilities.

This book is also for people in all roles of work organizations: managers, staff members, customers, suppliers, team leaders/members. Whatever your role, you'll find OTL ideas, guidelines, and examples that will help improve your person-to-person discussions about performance.

▲ A Final Note Before You Go On

On-The-Level communication may appear to be simple and seem like common sense, but it's often difficult and generally not common practice. As you and others around you build skills in this important area, be patient and understanding when communication doesn't go well. Strengthening communication practices is a never-ending process, an important part of ongoing personal development. We're very sensitive to that fact in this book and encourage you to take that message to heart. We firmly maintain, however, that anyone, in any role, can make dramatic improvements in the quality of his or her interactions through applying the principles and skills of On-The-Level communication.

PART I

Hallmarks of On-The-Level Communication

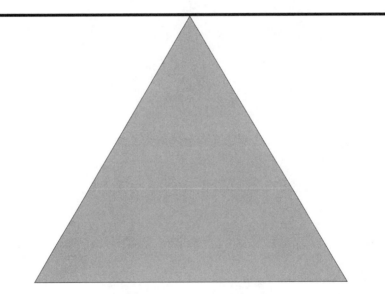

CHAPTER 1

What Is On-The-Level Communication?

Sam manages an engineering department in a manufacturing organization. He's been a technical specialist and a supervisor, and now he's the manager of engineering—quite a career! If you were to ask him what he thinks is the hardest part of being a manager, he would answer without hesitation:

"Talking with my team and team members about how we're doing. I guess I'm not comfortable either being a judge or getting personal feedback. A lot of these people have been my colleagues and friends for years. I'm afraid I usually avoid being direct and specific about what I think—whether it's giving compliments that might embarrass them or criticisms that might upset them."

Sara's an engineer in Sam's department. She's a senior project leader and has some specialized technical skills. Throughout her career, she's believed that good communication with her colleagues is essential to her own current perfor-mance as well as her

future opportunities. But performance-related communication from Sam has been sparse and mostly nonverbal. He simply hasn't given her much of an idea about how he views her performance—and she hasn't asked.

Each year, Sara thinks, "Well, my year-end performance feedback discussion is coming up. Maybe I'll get some insights there." But when the review comes, it's rushed, sandwiched between other performance discussions, which, like hers, must be completed before year's end. Sam's comments about Sara's performance aren't very specific and don't match the indirect messages she's been getting from him on a day-to-day basis. Frustrated, Sara begins to spend more time sulking at her desk and complaining to her colleagues about Sam's poor management practices.

Both Sam and Sara are having trouble communicating with each other about performance. What can they do to improve the situation?

▲ Performance Communication and Organizational Culture

In the past, the way organizations were designed—and thus, the roles people played in them—made performance communication difficult. Specifically, organizations were hierarchical and autocratic. This meant that authority and responsibility were held by a small group of managers who handed down decisions and policies to subordinates, who relied on this direction. Performance communication also followed this pattern, proceeding from the top down—rarely the other way around. In short, performance communication was not an *exchange* of ideas but rather a series of *directives*. And only a privileged few had the authority to initiate communication.

In recent years, many organizations have moved away from this rigid, hierarchical structure. Instead, they've adopted a more egalitarian arrangement, in which authority and responsibility are spread across the organization. The use of teams, mentioned throughout this book, is a good example of this new approach. These organizations still have managers and other people in positions of authority. But ideally, they serve more as *leaders* than *directors*. They seek the input of co-workers in making decisions and creating policies, which makes two-way communication vital.

Even within organizations working toward this more egalitarian structure, performance communication may be difficult. This may be especially true in the early days of change, before an open, comfortable atmosphere has been established. People may fall into old habits, playing superior or subordinate roles. Or they may simply be at a loss about how to communicate, even when encouraged to do so. Whatever the case, they need to learn a new approach to performance communication—one that works in all situations and for individuals at all levels of the organization.

▲ Guiding Principles of On-The-Level Communication

The On-The-Level (OTL) program meets these criteria. In effect, the OTL approach levels the performance communication "playing field," giving everyone the same tools and equivalent responsibilities.

OTL communication is characterized by four Guiding Principles:

- Directness
- Respect
- Shared responsibility
- Purpose

Let's consider each principle in turn.

Directness

Direct means "honest," "truthful." Direct is person to person. Direct performance communication is concrete and rich in information. It's descriptive, so all of us who are involved in the exchange have a com-

Guiding Principles of On-The-Level Communication

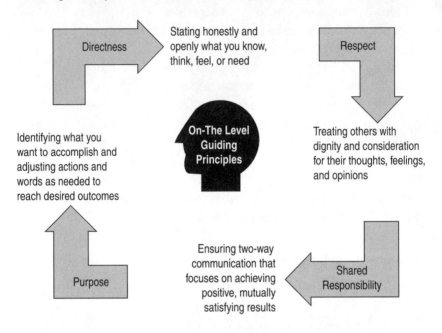

Directness
Stating honestly and openly what you know, think, feel, or need

Respect
Treating others with dignity and consideration for their thoughts, feelings, and opinions

On-The Level Guiding Principles

Identifying what you want to accomplish and adjusting actions and words as needed to reach desired outcomes

Purpose

Ensuring two-way communication that focuses on achieving positive, mutually satisfying results

Shared Responsibility

mon view of what it means. Direct communication is timely and candid. It's nonstrategic in the sense that we don't have any hidden intent to maneuver the communication for selfish gain.

Direct performance communication expresses what the sender really thinks and feels. But the message includes a humility that acknowledges the message may not be the objective truth. As direct communicators, we understand that personal biases affect what we feel and say, but we don't allow this to inhibit our expression. Rather, we see expressing the truth as a right, and we respectfully support that right for others as well as ourselves.

Directness both assumes and creates trust. Where there's fear, only people who are above fear (perhaps people in power) or who have great interpersonal courage and conviction (leaders, rebels, artists) communicate directly. Unfortunately, in many of these situations, directness leads to abuse and conflict. To prevent these destructive results, we all have to be willing to be direct and to expect directness, whatever our status or level of fear.

As organizations today try to become more productive, competitive, and creative, they must nurture directness. To do this, we have to leave behind years of autocracy, secrecy, mistrust, and fear. We also have to leave behind myths about how only people in power may say what they think. Part of the challenge of OTL is to nurture this shift toward directness—even if we must take small steps to get there.

Respect

OTL communicators deal with others respectfully—as people, not objects. They appreciate and consider others' needs, wants, and views, knowing that each of us brings unique gifts to the situation at hand.

As OTL communicators, part of the respect we show in performance situations is telling the truth as we see it. But telling the truth doesn't abuse or denigrate people or their ideas. The exchange is one in which "I'll tell you what I think, feel and see, but I am respectful of the you I'm telling. And I expect the same from you."

Respect requires that we listen to and acknowledge the views and feelings of others, taking their unique perspectives, commitments, histories, and values into account. In respectful interactions, we may disagree, but we don't embarrass, intimidate, correct, or attack unless our rights or ethics have been violated.

Underlying the notion of respect is the assumption that we are all worthwhile, possess special capabilities, and therefore have a right to our unique experiences and perspectives. None of us, by virtue of status or even special attributes, such as creativity, is entitled to more respect than anyone else.

Shared Responsibility

Both parties in performance communication today need to share responsibility for its success. It's no longer appropriate for managers to be responsible for communicating about such things as goals, feedback, and development, while staff members' roles remain passive or undefined. All of us—in all positions, at all levels of the organization—must own our jobs, increasing fulfillment and productivity for ourselves and our organizations.

Similarly, in supplier/customer relationships, suppliers should not take all the responsibility for communicating with customers. The associate who's closest to the customer and the production process will provide important information for goal setting. The customer will have a unique perspective on his or her own needs. And the manager who participates in strategy meetings will have a unique perspective on future skills requirements. Relationships that produce results are owned by all parties.

We all need to take responsibility for bringing our unique insights and perspectives to performance communication. Expecting people in authority to have all the answers is irresponsible, and expecting to have all the answers because of our own status is demagoguery. We're emerging from years of codependency in the workplace. In the past, we expected managers to do all the thinking in return for unquestioning loyalty. We expected workers to follow orders in return for continued employment and an old-age pension. We expected customers to take what they got. And we expected suppliers to negotiate prices following the motto "To the shrewd go the spoils."

This history of warped responsibility for performance communication has left quite a legacy: high cost structures, excessive waste, suspicion and blaming, and alienation of people from their leaders and suppliers from their customers. At the core of change is a simple truth: We must each play a responsible role in every performance communication situation. Failure to agree to goals and roles, to find and use feedback, and to learn and develop aren't our *individual* failures but rather our *collective* failures. We're all responsible for the situations we create. So in blaming others, we also point the finger at ourselves.

The lesson of shared responsibility in person-to-person communication is this: Unless we all commit to communication success and own our roles in being direct and respectful, new-age organizations and relationships won't materialize. We need to stop blaming the people "down there" for lack of motivation and the people "up there" for abuse of power. And we need to get on with building a workplace and world founded on shared responsibility.

Purpose

OTL communication isn't random or unfocused. It's conscious, intentional, and oriented to specific results—in other words, purposeful. When we communicate On-The-Level about performance, we want to reach agreement about goals and roles, to explore and use feedback, and to enhance and focus learning and development. In short, we want to make decisions and solve problems related to performance.

This doesn't mean that the purpose of a discussion won't change during its course. OTL discussions put information "on the table" that may change our perspectives on what we want to accomplish. But accomplishing *something* must always be the goal. We should intend to be closer to agreement as a result of our discussion. This may mean that we have a better understanding of issues, a clearer sense of options, or a greater level of trust among ourselves. It might mean that we have redefined the purpose or taken steps toward accomplishing it.

Whatever the case, OTL is intentional communication. That's one reason why directness, respect, and shared responsibility are so important. Deliberate performance communication must be grounded in these principles to ensure that it achieves the best results and does not lead to abuse.

▲ Person-to-Person Performance Communication

For the purposes of this book, OTL communication is dynamic, interactive communication about performance. It occurs between two people, voice to voice and face to face. It's a living process that happens in real time, between two people by themselves or between two people in a group. For this reason, in our definition of OTL, we'll exclude written and media-based communication, both of which are largely one way, even when opportunities to react have been built in.

Person-to-person performance communication, no matter how planned and responsible, always has elements of surprise. The surprise may occur because of different perceptions or purposes. For example, an innocuous word by one party may trigger a host of emotions and defensiveness in the other. New insights and options may be discovered during conversation that change the goals "in flight," so to speak.

Because of the dynamism and uncertainties inherent in performance communication, it's impossible to program an OTL conversation. All we can do is prepare as best we can, deeply commit to the principles of OTL (directness, respect, shared responsibility, and purpose), be conscious of what's happening in the discussion, and have a repertoire of skills to use in keeping things on track and On-The-Level.

An OTL conversation is like a dance. It may be a waltz (a *goals* discussion), a tango (a *feedback* discussion), or an extemporaneous ballet (a *development* discussion). The actual movement across the floor will depend on how skilled the partners are, how they react to each other, and what the music inspires.

▲ Where Do You Stand?

After the text discussion in each chapter, you'll have the opportunity to reflect on your performance communication practices, both strengths and weaknesses. Look at each "Where Do You Stand?" section as a sort of personal checklist, in which you evaluate your skills against the guidelines for OTL communication presented in the chapter.

Think about your own performance communication practices, as sender and as receiver. Consider the questions that follow, and evaluate where you stand:

- **As a sender, to what extent do you:**

  _____ Put aside fears and communicate what you really think and feel?

  _____ Present concrete, candid, and timely information?

  _____ Acknowledge that your message may not be objective, given personal biases, yet try not to maneuver the communication for selfish gain?

  _____ Consider others' needs, wants, and views?

  _____ Treat everyone as a unique individual, regardless of experience, creativity, or status?

  _____ Try to embarrass, intimidate, correct, or attack people who disagree with you?

  _____ Bring your unique insights and perspectives to performance communication?

  _____ See performance communication as an exchange, for which you have partial but not complete responsibility?

  _____ Accept that others have the right and responsibility to respond to you?

  _____ Communicate to achieve conscious, intentional, and specific results?

  _____ Flexibly adapt your purpose without losing sight of achieving some goal?

- **As a receiver, to what extent do you:**

  _____ Put aside fears and accept direct performance communication?

  _____ Listen intently to the message presented to understand the view of the sender?

  _____ Identify personal biases or agendas that may affect the objectivity of the message received?

  _____ Listen to and acknowledge the views and feelings of others, treating them as people, not objects?

_____ Treat everyone as a unique individual, regardless of experience, creativity, or status?

_____ Try to embarrass, intimidate, correct, or attack people who criticize or disagree with you?

_____ Bring your unique insights and perspectives to performance communication?

_____ See performance communication as an exchange, for which you have partial responsibility?

_____ Communicate to achieve conscious, intentional, and specific results?

_____ Flexibly adapt your purpose without losing sight of achieving some goal?

Based on your answers, what do you most want to improve about your roles as receiver and sender to make performance communication more On-The-Level?

▲ Key Points

- In the past, organizations were hierarchical and autocratic, such that performance communication (like authority and responsibility) was the domain of a small group of managers who handed down decisions and policies to subordinates, who relied on this direction.

- In recent years, many organizations have adopted a more egalitarian arrangement, in which authority and responsibility are spread across the organization. Input is sought from individuals at all levels, making two-way communication vital.

- OTL communication is characterized by directness, respect, shared responsibility, and purpose, all combined in person-to-person performance communication.

- Direct communication is concrete and rich in information, timely and candid, and as objective as possible (acknowledging that personal biases may enter in).

- Respectful communication considers the needs, wants, and views of others, treating them as people, not objects.

- Shared responsibility for communication means that both parties must bring their unique insights and perspectives to the exchange and accept partial responsibility for its success.

- Purposeful communication is conscious, intentional, and oriented to specific results.

- Person-to-person communication about performance, no matter how purposeful and responsible, always has elements of surprise; thus, it's impossible to program an OTL conversation.

- OTL communication is relevant to *all* workplace relationships: managers with staff members, staff members with each other, customers with suppliers.

CHAPTER 2

The On-The-Level Process: Six Communication Skills

Dave's a marketing manager in a major consumer products organization. He recently had a conversation with Laurie, his manager, about how to handle a difficult situation with a colleague from another department. After listening to Dave explain the situation, Laurie tried to advise him:

"Well, Dave, you're very clear about how Bill's way of working with marketing on this new product development project needs to change. Why don't you tell him exactly what you've just told me?"

"I know I should," Dave responded,

"but I never find the right moment. If I set a special meeting just to discuss this issue, it might blow the whole thing out of proportion. Besides, I know Bill's going to feel criticized no matter how I do this, and I can't afford to make our working together any more difficult."

Laurie paused for a moment and then pointed out that Dave's concern about how Bill would respond didn't show much confidence in his own ability to talk through the issue constructively. She asked Dave:

"What makes this situation any different than a tough negotiation with our advertising agency or pointing out problems with one of our promotions? I've seen you handle those situations effectively a hundred times. You're a very skilled communicator."

The vote of confidence from Laurie felt good, and as Dave got up to leave, he thanked her. He could acknowledge successful performance communication practices in many situations. Yet he didn't seem to know how to begin giving feedback to Bill. In looking back, he thought about how often his communication skills seemed to be automatic. When facing a difficult situation, it's easy to be self-conscious and suddenly not know what to do.

▲ On-The-Level Communication Skills

It's one thing to know what On-The-Level communication is but quite another to apply it regularly. To be able to communicate effectively in a variety of performance situations requires being aware of the fundamental principles and skills involved and feeling confident about using them.

In Chapter 1, we reviewed the four On-The-Level (OTL) Guiding Principles:

- Directness
- Respect
- Shared responsibility
- Purpose

Whereas these guiding principles reflect your intent in any discussion, the six OTL Communication Skills give you a kind of performance communication "tool kit" with which you can influence the outcome of the discussion. You select the "tool," or skill, that's most appropriate at each stage of the discussion.

Six skills are especially important in achieving OTL communication. Three of them—observing, listening, and empathizing—are **receptive skills.** That is, the person using these skills must be in a receptive, nonevaluative frame of mind in order to use them effectively. The other three—questioning, describing, and concluding—are **expressive skills.** The person using these skills needs to be in a proactive, risk-taking frame of mind.

All the expressive and receptive skills reflect the guiding principles of OTL communication. Specifically:

- Our ability to be *direct* depends on our expressive skills.

- Both expressive skills, which enlighten without blaming or judging, and receptive skills, which show understanding and consideration of the other person's point of view, help create mutual *respect.*

- *Shared responsibility* occurs when both people are willing and able to shift back and forth between expressive and receptive skills.

- When two people communicate, each has a *purpose* that needs to be articulated (expressed) and then understood (received) before differences can be resolved.

A careful balance between expressive and receptive skills is needed to accomplish OTL communication. Conscious awareness of

On-The-Level Communication Skills

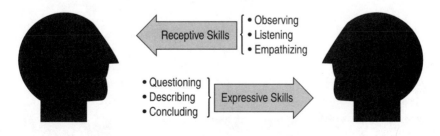

the skills used and the outcomes they can produce will help us stay alert to what's going on during an exchange.

We'll consider the six OTL Communication Skills in detail in the following sections: "Receptive Skills" and "Expressive Skills."

▲ Receptive Skills

There are three receptive skills: *observing, listening,* and *empathizing.* They're called *receptive* skills because they're used to receive information. Contrary to what some people assume, receptive skills are active, not passive, communication skills. They require making conscious choices to set aside other thoughts, block out distractions, and pay attention to the other person's ideas, thoughts, and feelings.

The need for receptive skills is important for effective performance communication, regardless of what your job is or what your work relationships might be. For instance, in a manager/staff member exchange, it's a mistake for the manager to assume that he or she should use primarily expressive skills and the staff member, primarily receptive skills. In effective On-The-Level communication, both parties receive and express in a reasonably balanced way.

As you read about each receptive skill, look over the list of "Key Behaviors," which offers concrete examples of the skill being used. Also review the statement about the "Intended Outcome," which gives the effect of using the skill appropriately. Finally, think about your own practices when you're trying to communicate On-The-Level. The section "Putting It Into Practice" identifies potential biases and difficulties and suggests how to avoid them.

Observing

Observing is acting on the choice to look at what's happening, to detect consequences of actions, and to notice whether what's happening is unique or part of a pattern.

KEY BEHAVIORS

- Notice what's happening in and across situations.
- Recognize specific examples of behavior—things someone does or says in a particular situation—that either confirm or deny more general conclusions about his or her actions or style.
- Detect accurate patterns in behaviors and results.

INTENDED OUTCOME

To get accurate and specific information about behavior, feelings, patterns of behavior, and results

PUTTING IT INTO PRACTICE

The skill of observing depends on seeing and hearing accurately and resisting the temptation to make assumptions, interpretations, or judgments about a person's behavior. The goal is to heighten awareness of data without prematurely deciding what it means. We need to be conscious of our positive and negative reactions in order to control attitudes and judgments about what we see and hear.

One type of mental filter that can inhibit skilled observing is *haloing,* which refers to letting positive or negative general reactions to a person affect interpretations of what he or she says or does. Putting a positive "halo" on someone results in unconsciously choosing to see only positive actions and qualities, ignoring the negative. An example of this sort of haloing is the star staff member who seems to do no wrong. Putting a negative "halo" on someone leads to searching for examples of behavior that support negative assumptions about him or her, overlooking any positive behavior. An example of negative haloing is the associate who makes one very visible error and subsequently has every piece of work scrutinized, every idea questioned. This can be particularly debilitating because when people look for problems, they tend to find them. Haloing, then, can cause selective observing, where we look for specific types of things or prematurely stop observing, assuming there's nothing more to see.

Another obstruction to observing is *stereotyping.* We stereotype when we react to people based on preconceptions about the groups we think they represent. Stereotypes based on sex, race, and age are the most common examples in society and the workplace, and it's dangerously easy to jump to conclusions. Often, people aren't even aware of the categories they've established in their minds or how they slot people into these groups. In order to observe effectively, it's necessary to resist the tendency to form either positive or negative conclusions that aren't founded on firsthand data.

Projection, another type of bias, occurs when we transfer our own fears, assumptions, and beliefs to other people. We project our own feelings and reactions onto the other person, as if he or she were a movie screen. Instead of seeing the other person's behavior accurately, we filter what we observe through assumptions based on our own projected motives, feelings, or thoughts. Even if people are similar in one way, they won't necessarily be similar in other ways. We can't afford to stop observing too soon. A skillful observer identifies specific examples of another person's behavior that are relevant to the issue at hand, rather than simply making guesses or assumptions about what that person intends to do.

Listening

Listening is hearing what has been said or implied, detecting the key points and issues presented, and checking the accuracy of what has been heard.

KEY BEHAVIORS
- Clear your mind and focus on the other person's words and intended meaning.
- Paraphrase and/or ask questions to confirm your understanding.
- Detect the feelings and thoughts of others accurately.

INTENDED OUTCOME
To get mutual clarity and understanding, regardless of whether both parties agree

PUTTING IT INTO PRACTICE

Listening requires consciously deciding to be a receiver. The goal of listening is to *understand* another person's observations and reactions as well as what he or she wants or needs. Reaching this understanding is obviously difficult when there are differences between you and the other person. Even when you're able to shift into using the skill of active listening, staying with it long enough can be difficult when the other person in the interaction has strong feelings and complex thoughts. We tend to interrupt with our own reactions and rebuttals before fully hearing out and understanding the other person.

The biases described earlier that can inhibit skilled observing can equally disrupt skilled listening. We may hear selectively or incorrectly when others present their points of view because we have made prejudgments or assumptions. We can take two steps to guard against these blocks to effective listening:

1. *Consciously decide to listen in order to understand*—This clearing of the mind fosters accurate hearing. You need to consciously decide to be curious about the other person's point of view.

2. *Paraphrase to check for understanding*—A person with a strong investment in asserting a point of view may find it difficult to paraphrase. He or she may believe that restating another person's point of view implies agreement with it. In order to listen effectively, we need to see that understanding different points of view is not the same as agreeing with them. Paraphrasing ensures that our biases have not distorted the other person's perspective and that the commitment to accurate understanding communicates respect.

On-The-Level communication involves an exchange of receptive and expressive stances. If one party isn't committed to listening to the other's point of view, he or she can't expect reciprocal commitment when presenting his or her own view. The ability to resolve differences is based on the assumption that both people are working to understand each other. Effective listening isn't just a matter of skillfully executing behaviors that *look* like listening. It means making the choice to be receptive for the purpose of understanding the other person.

Empathizing

Empathizing is detecting another person's feelings and values and validating a common understanding of them.

KEY BEHAVIORS

- Acknowledge and accept the thoughts, feelings, values, and opinions of others.
- Communicate your understanding of the thoughts, feelings, values, and opinions of others.
- Share similar experiences that demonstrate your understanding.

INTENDED OUTCOME

To reduce tension and enhance trust and sharing

PUTTING IT INTO PRACTICE

Empathizing is a natural follow-up to listening. Listening focuses on information, such as data, ideas, and analysis. Listening also involves a search of experiences, feelings, and values that add perspective, intensity, and importance to the information the other person is expressing. To listen fully, we need to attend to the other person at both the level of information and the level of feelings and values. Empathizing is the skill of overtly validating the experiences, feelings, and values that have been observed or heard.

Common experiences, values, and feelings that aren't expressed don't create empathy. The outcome of skilled empathizing won't happen until both parties share a common ground. Some of the ways this can happen include:

- Sharing an experience or reaction that's similar to what another person has had
- Providing an example that embodies or illustrates the feelings or values the other person has described
- Using an analogy to represent the feelings or values the other person has described
- When the two people know each other well, making an acknowledging nonverbal gesture or nod

Like any of the skills, effective empathizing requires both the ability to do it *and* the ability to know when to do it. Showing empathy over an issue that's relatively unimportant might be considered by others as patronizing. On the other hand, failing to stop and validate someone's reaction when it's both important to him or her and relevant to the issue being discussed can cause that person to pull out of the discussion.

It's difficult, if not impossible, to empathize when the other person's experiences, feelings, or values are totally different from your own. At the very least, however, when you respectfully acknowledge that the other person has strongly held experiences, feelings, and values, you'll help keep the channels of communication open.

▲ Expressive Skills

There are three expressive skills: *questioning, describing,* and *concluding.* These proactive skills are necessary to add information and direction to a discussion. As stated earlier, effective On-The-Level communication requires a balanced use of receptive and expressive skills. Receptive skills provide the mutual understanding that's a necessary foundation to an effective OTL discussion, and expressive skills add the information and direction that are helpful in resolving or reaching conclusions to the issues being discussed.

As you read about each of the three expressive skills, think about your own communication practices.

Questioning

Questioning is asking for information and opinions in a way that gets relevant, honest, and appropriately detailed responses.

KEY BEHAVIORS

- Form questions in response to what's being said.
- Ask questions to confirm or gather information.
- Ask open-ended questions rather than closed, or "yes/no," questions.

INTENDED OUTCOME

To bring relevant information into the discussion and prevent misunderstanding

PUTTING IT INTO PRACTICE

Questioning is an expressive skill because questions create focus and direction and reduce road blocks in a conversation. Questions uncover information so everyone can use it. Taking time to ask questions gives both parties an opportunity to explore observations and conclusions. It also provides the time to reflect, which can reduce tension and minimize the risk of jumping to early conclusions about where another person stands.

The purpose of questioning is to probe proactively. A mechanical sensing device, like a temperature probe, is a good analogy. It has only one purpose: to collect information. It doesn't judge or evaluate. The goal of effective questioning is to get relevant information out in the open. If the other person hears a negative judgment in the way a question is asked or if that person senses that the questioner is trying to back up an already formed negative opinion, he or she may shut down communication or at least become defensive.

The skill of questioning is particularly important when each person in a discussion has moved quickly to express a position and the differences between the two are significant. Simply restating positions in this type of situation won't help. Asking questions, however, will continue the search for other ways to resolve differences because it focuses on the possibility that some helpful information still has not been uncovered.

Questioning also plays a unique role as a *transition skill* for moving from an expressive to a receptive role in communication—for example, asking, "What do you think about what I've just suggested?" After asking this type of question, the individual needs to use effective listening skills to complete the communication.

Questioning, at its best, requires:

- Being interested in what the other person says and showing that interest both in words and nonverbal communication, such as facial expressions and posture

- Asking open-ended questions, which prompt exploration, rather than closed questions, which prompt limited responses ("yes" or "no")

Look at the following examples of both types of questions. In each pair, the questions would be asked for essentially the same purpose but would produce highly different answers:

Closed-Ended Questions	Open-Ended Questions
– Can you say more about that?	– What else can you say about that?
– Do you think we have any options?	– What options do you think we have?
– Were you upset when that happened?	– How did you feel when that happened?
– Can you describe the results that occurred?	– In your view, what results occurred?

Clearly, the open-ended questions get much more and relevant information than the closed-ended questions do. What's more, open-ended questions keep the conversation going, whereas closed-ended questions shut it down.

Describing

Describing is identifying concrete, specific examples of behavior and its effects.

KEY BEHAVIORS
- Provide appropriate detail of specific actions and behaviors to clarify the focus of discussion.
- Provide examples of specific actions and behaviors in order to show how they influence results or affect other people.
- Ensure that the timing and amount of detail of examples of behavior and its effects are appropriate.

INTENDED OUTCOME
To ensure that both parties reach a concrete and common understanding of the issues being discussed

PUTTING IT INTO PRACTICE
It's easy to overlook describing as an important skill in effective communication. It may seem obvious that people who want to have an On-The-Level discussion will make specific observations and identify the effects of what they've observed—in other words, that they'll describe. The problem isn't that people don't understand the importance of descriptive communication. It's that people often don't realize that they're not being clear and accurate in what they say. This happens because the human mind jumps so quickly to generalizations and judgments.

For instance, Jan, one of Peter's colleagues, wants to give him supportive performance communication. She may not realize that she's sending an incomplete message when she says, "Peter, you're really a great team player, and I like working with you on this project." Peter will understand that Jan appreciates something, but it won't be clear *what* that specific something is. Unless Jan gives a description that includes examples of what Peter actually did and how it influenced others and the meeting itself, Peter won't know why he's being acknowledged. He also won't know specifically what to do in the future to have further success.

The performance communication would be more descriptive and useful if Jan said something like this:

"Peter, in yesterday's project meeting, you helped us resolve a team conflict. You really listened, asked questions, and drew conclusions that helped us settle our differences. I like working with you on this project."

In this message, Jan is clear about exactly what Peter did that she appreciated. She mentions specific behaviors and results. Not only will this message make more sense to Peter, but he will know what to do for continued success.

The ability to be specific rather than general is even more crucial when discussing a problem or concern about someone's actions. Using generalizations that suggest negative judgments produces strong defensive reactions. For instance, consider the following statements:

"You're unprofessional."
"You've never been able to follow through on your commitments."

These statements are both judgmental. The label *unprofessional* and use of the word *never* are interpretations, not specific data.

A descriptive statement, which is anchored in a specific incident or event, will sound more like this:

"When X happened, I heard you say Y, and the effect was Z."

Specific, concrete examples give important support to any conclusions reached by either person in a conversation. For instance, suppose that Hector, a manager, has reached the conclusion that Jane, a staff member, doesn't have enough of a "sense of urgency." In order for Jane to understand what Hector means, he will have to provide a specific, descriptive example. Hector might say:

"In yesterday's project review meeting, you said we were behind on our schedule without stating an action plan for recovering lost time and meeting delivery dates."

Use of a descriptive example gives the communication substance and credibility. Doing so also creates a clear context for identifying how Hector will expect Jane's behavior to change: Hector wants Jane to provide contingency plans that demonstrate firm commitment to delivery dates.

Whenever we want to react to or influence another person's behavior, examples and clear observations give discussions substance and meaning.

Concluding

Concluding is articulating and clarifying overall positions, recommendations, and decisions.

KEY BEHAVIORS
- Assess and determine the overall quality of observed behaviors and results.
- Control personal biases.
- Separate what is in someone's control and what is not.
- State specific consequences, decisions, or recommendations.

INTENDED OUTCOME
To reach understanding between senders and receivers about where they stand in terms of overall positions, recommendations, decisions, agreements, and potential consequences

PUTTING IT INTO PRACTICE
Concluding works hand in hand with describing. Concrete, specific examples of behavior and its effects ought to be cited as the basis for evaluations, recommendations, and decisions. When concluding is done unilaterally, without the benefit of the other person's participation, it shuts down communication. But when concluding is done in a way that respects the needs and rights of the other person and is based on joint input, it leads to real progress toward resolution and action.

When we conclude, we assess the information available and give both the criteria for our conclusion as well as the conclusion itself. We also name and explore any biases and assumptions that may affect our conclusions.

Sometimes, the conclusion that one person reaches in a discussion will be similar to that reached by another. In this case, it's relatively easy to complete the discussion and get ready for action. When the conclusions reached by two people are significantly different, however, the skill of concluding feels much riskier.

In a performance discussion among peers, for example, two people from different departments might agree on something that's happened and its effects. But if the goals for the two departments are different, the two parties might reach dramatically different conclusions about what to do next. Whether it's a manager/staff member relationship or a peer relationship, differences can only be resolved after people have talked about their positions and recommendations and how they see the consequences of various options.

When you have the ultimate responsibility regarding a particular topic or within a team or department, you might appropriately use all the receptive and expressive skills to ensure a thorough discussion. Regardless of whether others agree with you, as the person in charge, you have the clear responsibility to bring the discussion to a conclusion. That means making decisions and being clear about consequences for not following those decisions.

▲ Staying Alert to Skill Outcomes

The six OTL Communication Skills are like tools. Each skill, when used effectively and at the right time, produces visible outcomes. But strengths in some skill areas don't substitute for weaknesses in others. Being skilled in listening and empathizing skills, for example, will make you effective when those skills are appropriate, but it won't make up for deficiencies in describing and concluding skills. Similarly, overusing expressive skills and avoiding receptive skills will lead to ineffective communication.

Consider an exchange in which one person seems upset and needs to express his or her point of view. What should the other person—the receiver—do? As an effective communicator, the receiver would use the skill of *listening* to understand the first person's thoughts and feelings. Then, the receiver would paraphrase in order to demonstrate his or her understanding. Listening, however, isn't complete until a noticeable outcome has resulted. In this case, the initial desired outcome is to reduce the emotional tension. Until this happens, constructive communication for another purpose won't occur.

If early attempts at listening don't reduce the tension, then the effective communicator might try the skill of listening again. If listening is successful this time, then the receiver should move on to a different skill, such as *empathizing*. Or if it seems appropriate, the receiver should use *questioning* in order to explore and gather more information relevant to the purpose of the discussion.

Many people find that the receptive skills are easier for them and the expressive skills are more challenging, or vice versa. Throughout our lives, most of us have probably had mixed results when we've used these skills. An important first step in improving these communication outcomes is to know that different skills will improve the effectiveness of performance communication when used in various combinations. Effective OTL communication requires practicing all the skills and building confidence in using them consciously and shifting from one skill to another, as appropriate.

▲ Communication Games

On-The-Level communication is made much more difficult when, for a variety of reasons, people avoid being direct with each other. Sometimes, being direct is discouraged by cultural norms. Other times, an issue may be avoided because it's unimportant. Most often, however, we avoid being direct because of fear or anxiety about the consequences. When this happens, we may take refuge in communication games.

Even when both people in a conversation effectively use the six communication skills, games can be significant barriers to OTL communication. These diversions to communication are called *games* because the message to be communicated goes underground, other dynamics and agendas take over, and the participants have to guess at what the real message is.

Everyone plays these games at some time, whether as a communication receiver or sender. It's important to be able to recognize games and to know when they're being played, for there are ways to stop them before they seriously interfere with what you're trying to accomplish.

See if you recognize yourself or others in the games described in the following sections. Then, the next time you observe these games or others like them being played, stand back, assess the situation, and bring the discussion back to a more direct exchange.

Sender Games

When someone needs to share information or state a position but decides to be indirect, rather than use the skills of questioning, describing, and concluding, he or she is playing a sender's communication game. Here are some examples:

It's My Duty is a game of obligation. The message sender might say, "Well, I owe it to you to tell you this . . ." and then proceed to deliver the message as if he or she doesn't believe it's true. For instance, a manager might begin a performance discussion by saying, "Here we go again, having to do another one of these reviews," suggesting that the two people are just going through the motions to satisfy a requirement, rather than having a meaningful conversation. For the receiver, this game creates a cold, impersonal, and peripheral experience; he or she is unlikely to ask questions or attempt to solve problems. The sender might use this game to protect himself or herself from a possible defensive response from the receiver, but the result is that neither person takes the interaction seriously.

Junk Dealer is a game in which the message is buried with qual-
ifiers, reservations, or irrelevant information. For instance, an individual might preface a criticism with a statement such as, "You

don't have to agree with this, and
you might want to check this out
for yourself. After all, it's just my
view, you know, and I am only
basing this on limited data . . ."
By the time the sender gets to
the point, the "trash" around it
has covered the message. The
result is that the receiver has a
difficult time first understanding and then knowing how to
interpret the importance of the
message. As in the game It's My Duty, the sender is creating a "back
door" to escape through, in case the receiver responds in a negative
way.

Life Saver is a game that attempts to protect the receiver from the
message. It's a paternalistic tactic. Sometimes, after communicating

something that causes the receiver to become defensive, the
sender will throw him or her a
"life saver": "Well, don't worry
about it. It's really just a little
thing I thought I should bring to
your attention." In effect, the
sender "back pedals" to try to
make up for saying something
the receiver didn't want to hear.
The result is an inaccurate impression of the importance of the
message.

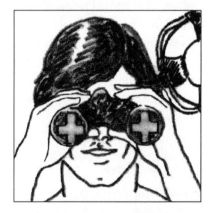

Detective is a game of asking leading questions. Rather than coming out and stating a position or point of view, the sender asks questions that are often closed (answered "yes" or "no") and that imply an opinion without saying it: "Did you really think that would work?" or "Wasn't it clear from my request that you should've tried a different ap-  proach?" This game makes the receiver defensive because it implies a judgment. The sender would do better to clearly state her or his expectations or thoughts on performance.

The truth is, we all avoid being direct at times. The best antidote to sender games is to realize this and use the expressive skills more effectively. When using questioning, for example, make sure your purpose is truly to gather information, not to give a veiled opinion. Describing and concluding skills will help you say what you have to say without beating around the bush or minimizing the message.

Remember, you can't control how someone else responds to what you say. So just say it, let the receiver respond, and if difficulty results, try to resolve it *when it actually happens.* Many times, people use sender communication games because they're anticipating problems that may never actually happen.

Receiver Games

People who receive messages use diversion tactics, too. Perhaps they suspect they're about to hear something they don't want to hear and use receiver games to head off the communication. Here are a few games receivers play:

Wounded Animal is a game of making the sender feel guilty. The receiver interprets the situation as being far more negative than the sender intends and reflects this view by looking hurt or by pouting or sulking. This response may start a chain reaction of games. For

example, if the sender thinks that the receiver can't take the information, he or she might soothe the situation with the Life Saver game (discussed earlier). If this happens, both the sender and receiver will successfully prevent getting any constructive outcome. OTL communication isn't possible if the receiver doesn't take responsibility for hearing the message. If the sender is

using OTL skills effectively, he or she will communicate the message in a responsible way and not have to take care of the receiver. The result of Wounded Animal is that the receiver not only misses what may be important information but also discovers that the people around him or her avoid direct communication.

Change the Scent is a game of diversion. Here, rather than checking for understanding or asking for more details, the receiver quickly changes the subject. For example, when a customer calls to discuss shipping delays with product X, the supplier might sidestep this

topic and talk about shipments of other products instead. By doing so, the supplier avoids having a productive discussion with the customer, one in which they would explore issues and draw conclusions about the problem raised. This game succeeds if the sender stops trying to bring the discussion back to the main point.

Counterattack is a game of defending oneself at all costs. It's the ultimate in defensiveness: The receiver initiates the attack before hearing and exploring the information or position being expressed by the sender. The receiver counters with remarks such as these: "You're being unreasonable, as usual," "The real problem is that *you're* handling the situation," or "But *you* do the same thing you're saying *I* do." Counterattack shifts the receiver into an expressive and blaming role when he or she should be listening to and understanding the message instead. This game breaks down the listening process and makes it impossible to explore the issue at hand.

Ally Building is a game of "safety in numbers." It comes into play when the receiver gets as many people on his or her side as possible in order to build a case for rejecting the sender's message. After garnering

this support, the receiver can say, "Well, nobody else believes that" or "I've asked a lot of other people who work here, and they don't see it like you do." This game helps the receiver avoid listening to and acting on information from the sender. It also demeans and discounts the sender's message before it's even understood. Although it's appropriate to check out opinions, using experiences with others to defend oneself in a difficult situation prevents getting effective results in communication.

Receivers can avoid playing these games if they choose instead to observe, listen, and empathize. Most receiver games are "smoke screens" put in place to avoid getting a message or taking an action. Sometimes, a receiver may be playing a game (like one of those described here) but be unaware of it. In this case, the sender needs to bring attention to what's happening, just as the receiver might have to call attention to a sender game.

For example, if the sender is playing Life Saver, the receiver might say:

> *"You're trying to tell me something important. You don't have to gloss over it to protect my feelings. Tell me what you think."*

Or if the receiver is playing Ally Building, the sender might say:

> *"I recognize that your experience with others has been different than mine. Please listen to my point about this situation."*

Recognizing and identifying what's happening is the first step in getting back to OTL communication. The next step is to replace communication games with the six skills of observing, listening, empathizing, questioning, describing, and concluding, as they're needed in an interaction.

If you work in an organization or a social culture in which direct communication isn't encouraged, you may choose to create your own subculture within the group or team you work with most directly. You can make this happen by having frank discussions about what On-The-Level communication is and how different it is from other ways of communicating. It may take awhile before people feel safe enough to try OTL. But with encouragement, training in appropriate skills, and support for taking risks to be direct, you can increase the quality of performance communication among the people in your workplace.

▲ Keeping the Human Element

Always remember that performance communication occurs between two human beings. Thus, it's always a partially subjective process that can't be mechanized or substituted by a form or a script. Performance communication is most meaningful when it's engaged in face to face and the parties have made a personal commitment to being On-The-Level: using the four guiding principles, applying the six skills, and avoiding communication games.

▲ Where Do You Stand?

The communication games reviewed in this chapter illustrate the bad habits many of us fall into when we lack the skills for effective performance communication. But when provided with the "tool kit" of OTL skills, we have the means to develop new, more effective communication practices for a variety of situations.

Think about your own performance communication practices, as sender and as receiver. Consider the questions that follow, and evaluate where you stand:

- **As a sender, to what extent do you:**

    _____ Adopt a proactive, risk-taking frame of mind in applying the expressive skills: questioning, describing, and concluding?

    _____ Ask questions to confirm or gather information?

    _____ Use open-ended questions to prompt exploration, rather than closed-ended questions, which draw limited responses?

    _____ Provide appropriate details of specific actions and behaviors to clarify the focus of the discussion?

    _____ Provide details of actions and behaviors in order to indicate how they influence results or people?

    _____ Jump to generalizations and make judgments?

    _____ Control personal biases?

    _____ Identify and name assumptions?

    _____ Assess the overall quality of observed behaviors and results?

_____ Separate what is and is not under an individual's control?

_____ Respect the needs and rights of others and welcome their input in drawing conclusions?

_____ Accept the responsibility for bringing the discussion to a conclusion by making decisions and clarifying consequences?

_____ Play communication games by avoiding directness or trying to control how someone will respond?

- **As a receiver, to what extent do you:**

  _____ Adopt a receptive, nonevaluative frame of mind in applying the receptive skills: observing, listening, and empathizing?

  _____ Observe what's happening in and across situations?

  _____ Identify accurate patterns in behaviors and results?

  _____ Consciously examine personal biases and values and how they may affect your interpretations of what you see and hear?

  _____ Clear your mind and focus on both the thoughts and feelings delivered?

  _____ Paraphrase and/or ask questions to confirm your understanding?

  _____ Hear out the sender and not interrupt with your own reactions or rebuttals?

  _____ Listen to the other's point of view and expect him or her to do the same?

  _____ Acknowledge and accept the thoughts, feelings, values, and opinions of others?

  _____ Communicate your understanding of the thoughts, feelings, values, and opinions of others?

  _____ Share similar experiences or examples, make gestures, or otherwise demonstrate your understanding of the message?

_____ Ask questions in response to what's being said?

_____ Play communication games to head off information you don't want to hear, perhaps out of denial?

Based on your answers, what do you most want to improve about your roles as receiver and sender to make communication more On-The-Level?

▲ Key Points

- The six OTL Communication Skills provide a kind of communication "tool kit" with which you can influence the outcome of the discussion, selecting the "tool," or skill, most appropriate at each stage.
- The receptive skills are used to receive information; however, they're active, not passive, communication skills.
  - Observing is acting on the choice to look at what's happening, to detect consequences of actions, and to notice whether what's happening is unique or part of a pattern.
  - Listening is hearing what has been said or implied, detecting the key points and issues presented, and checking the accuracy of what has been heard.
  - Empathizing is detecting another person's feelings and values and validating a common understanding of them.
- Expressive skills are proactive skills that are necessary to add information and direction to a discussion.
  - Questioning is asking for information and opinions in a way that gets relevant, honest, and appropriately detailed responses.
  - Describing is identifying concrete, specific examples of behavior and its effects.
  - Concluding is articulating and clarifying overall positions, recommendations, and decisions.
- A careful balance among expressive and receptive skills is needed to accomplish OTL communication: Receptive skills provide the mutual understanding that's a necessary foundation to an effective OTL discussion, and expressive skills add the information and direction that are helpful in resolving or reaching conclusions to the issues being discussed.
- On-The-Level communication is much more difficult when people play games and avoid being direct with each other.
- Performance communication is most meaningful when it's presented face to face and a personal commitment has been made to being On-The-Level.

CHAPTER 3

Being an Observing Participant

Leslie, Bob's manager, tends to look over his shoulder to see if he's doing tasks delegated to him correctly. Because of this tendency, Bob anticipates that Leslie will "micromanage" a recently delegated project.

When Leslie greeted Bob on Tuesday morning, she asked how he was progressing on the new project. In spite of the angry knot in his stomach, Bob smiled and said, "Fine. In fact, I'll have a detailed progress report for you by Friday."

After Leslie walked away, Bob thought, "Great! Now I have to do that report just to keep her off my back."

On Friday, when Leslie got Bob's report, she wondered, "Why is he including so many small details? This worries me. He may not really understand the larger purpose of this project. Maybe I need to talk to him again."

And so a needless cycle of concern and wasted effort continues, as Leslie and Bob blindly confirm assumptions about each other's intent and performance. A little communication would go a long way in improving their results and their relationship.

▲ Recognizing the Power of the Observing Participant

Previous chapters presented On-The-Level (OTL) communication in terms of four Guiding Principles (directness, respect, shared responsibility, and purpose) and six Communication Skills (observing, listening, empathizing, questioning, describing, and concluding). But there's more to effective performance communication than demonstrating proficiency in using these principles and skills. Knowing *when* to use the skills, in particular, is also essential to communicating On-The-Level.

Assuming the role of an **Observing Participant** will give you that insight. Specifically, conscious use of the Observing Participant will help you stay aware of what's happening in a conversation while it's going on in order to:

1. Think about the purpose of the interaction and then
2. Choose the communication skills that will keep the discussion on track

Think of the Observing Participant as a type of self-talk—that dialogue that goes on inside your head, especially when you're trying to sort things out. When focused on performance communication, this dialogue makes you think about the implications of what's going on before, during, and after an important conversation.

We all use self-talk but not always in the most helpful ways. For example, think about how you might anticipate conflict in an upcoming meeting. Perhaps on the way to work, on the bus or in your car, you play out the conversation you expect to have. In your mind's eye, you see yourself stating your point, and you conjure up the response you fear most. Then, on the return trip at the end of the day, your mind drifts to a postmortem of the conversation. You decide that you liked some of what you said and did, but you think more about what went wrong. Your feelings about the person, the situation, and your own choices and behaviors well up inside you. And in the end, you judge yourself harshly, punishing yourself for being less effective than you'd like to have been.

Sound familiar? In these cases of preconversation anxiety and postconversation self-judgment, the focus is on fear and disappointment. And once these emotions have taken over, it's difficult to draw on communication skills, such as describing or active listening, that might lead to a successful conclusion. What's needed is some way to turn things around when the conversation starts to get off track.

Use of the Observing Participant helps you gain that control at any point in a conversation. Before the discussion, the Observing Participant helps you form a clear purpose and identify how to get started in a constructive way. During the conversation, the Observing Participant provides a self-correcting monitor that helps you stay on purpose. And after the conversation, the Observing Participant guides you to learn from the experience, thinking about what took place and deciding what the most constructive next step might be, if the communication hasn't been completed.

The spontaneity of human interaction increases the challenge of On-The-Level communication. Even when we take the time to plan what we intend to say, once we're in the conversation, unexpected things usually happen—not only because of the other person but also because of ourselves. Feelings, opinions, and even decisions that seemed clear yesterday can be called into question today, in the moment of interaction. The shift may be rational, perhaps based on hearing new information, or it may be irrational, rooted entirely in emotion.

Emotion always complicates communication. It follows, then, that the most difficult performance communication situations are those that come as a surprise. Consider these examples: Mike told his manager, Scott, for some time that everything was fine and then, in a burst of pent-up emotion, suddenly revealed that he'd been frustrated for months. Similarly, after reading a project proposal, Connie blasted Brett with criticism based on her misreading of his intentions. In situations such as these, the communication exchange resembles a punch in the stomach. You're caught completely unaware, and it takes you a moment or two to recover.

The Observing Participant helps you mentally step aside from an immediate emotional reaction and more objectively sense and explore what's happening in the conversation. Doing so makes the difference between a response that's automatic and defensive, shutting down communication, and one that keeps the channels open, creating constructive dialogue.

The Observing Participant also provides a useful check of our purpose in communication. In any ongoing relationship, whether at work or in our personal lives, we have to balance our immediate, momentary reactions with our long-term intentions. For instance, Denise, an experienced peer, decided to play the role of mentor to Nikolai, a new co-worker. When Nikolai interrupts Denise, she's sometimes irritated by his questions. Then she remembers what it's like to be new and that it's part of her role as mentor to take the time to listen and respond patiently. By engaging her Observing Participant, Denise is able put aside her initial reactions, remind herself of her purpose in the interaction, and respond in a manner that helps accomplish that purpose.

▲ The "STOP" and "SEE" Model

To recognize and practice the Observing Participant, you need to understand the steps involved in the process. The "STOP" and "SEE" Model outlines those steps. Once you realize a conversation is moving off purpose:

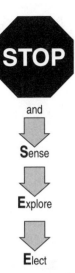

STOP

Mentally stop yourself for a moment to see what's really going on.

and

Sense

Consciously realize what you and the other person are thinking and feeling.

Explore

Think about what you want out of the conversation—your purpose—and how what you are sensing might affect this.

Elect

Given the situation, choose one or more of the six communication skills, and then use them to stay on purpose.

How to "STOP"

Each element of the "STOP" and "SEE" Model leads to the next, which means that realizing you need to take the first step is often the most challenging part. The first step is called "STOP" because the idea is to stop those mental mechanisms that put you on "automatic pilot" and then *consciously* guide your behavior in the conversation.

What most people experience when they try to engage the Observing Participant is that the opportunity for action has passed; that is, they mentally "STOP" and "SEE" too late. Consider the following case of an individual who became aware of a specific behavior he wanted to change:

Ben realized that he fired off sarcastic comments like bullets every time someone tried to communicate to him about his performance. At first, he found that even though he was aware of this behavior, he didn't realize he'd done it until he'd made the comment and seen the stunned look on the other person's face.

Eventually, he became aware of making sarcastic responses while delivering them, but he was unable to prevent himself from slipping into this old behavior. He had successfully observed himself and the interaction but wasn't able to stop early enough and try a new behavior. At this point, Ben was pretty discouraged about being able to change his habit, but he kept trying.

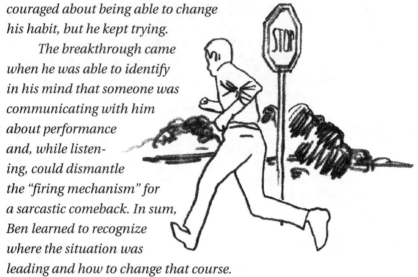

The breakthrough came when he was able to identify in his mind that someone was communicating with him about performance and, while listening, could dismantle the "firing mechanism" for a sarcastic comeback. In sum, Ben learned to recognize where the situation was leading and how to change that course.

Ben's experience illustrates that it takes conscious practice to "wake up" the Observing Participant early enough in the conversation to make better choices for performance communication. Here are some suggestions for learning how to "STOP":

- After a difficult interaction, particularly one in which you feel you didn't make the best choices, mentally review what happened and try to determine what triggered your reaction.
- Once you understand the words or behaviors that trigger unproductive patterns, develop some cues that will alert you to step aside mentally, early in the conversation.
- Be patient. Remember that learning how to "STOP" earlier and earlier in your conversations will happen gradually.
- If you make progress but then slip back into an old pattern you want to change, don't get discouraged. Review the experience, and use it as a reminder to redouble your efforts at change.

As an illustration, let's return to the Bob and Leslie scenario from the beginning of this chapter and replay the situation, using the Observing Participant. As you may recall, Bob and Leslie are stuck in a frustrating and unproductive cycle: Bob feels that Leslie overmanages him, constantly checking up on his work, and Leslie worries about Bob's ability to see the "big picture," since he seems caught up in details. Their self-talk indicates they're both anxious about the work and their relationship, but they aren't able to communicate their concerns effectively.

Here's what an effective "STOP" might look like in Bob's case. After Leslie's morning greeting and question about the status of the new project, Bob's Observing Participant says:

> *"I can't believe this. I haven't had this assignment 24 hours, and already there's an inquisition! OK, cool down."*

Leslie notices Bob's surprised look in response to her question, and her Observing Participant says:

> *"Whoops! It looks like I've stepped on a land mine. I wonder why?"*

By listening to their self-talk, Bob and Leslie have stopped their natural tendencies to go on "automatic pilot." Engaging their Observing Participants has helped them recognize that the conversation has the potential to get off track from the original purpose and intent. They have "STOPPED." The next step is to "Sense" what's going on— with themselves and one another.

How to "Sense"

If the first step of this process, "STOP," is a wake-up call to conscious awareness, then the second step, "Sense," involves really noticing and mentally naming what we take in. We all have thoughts and feelings when we anticipate an interaction, while it's going on, and after we complete it. But we're not only focusing on ourselves.

Whether we realize it or not, we're also focusing on others:

- First, anticipating their reactions
- Then, hearing their words and noting their nonverbal cues during the conversation
- And finally, after the conversation, reviewing our impression of their thoughts and feelings

"Sensing" involves understanding as much as we can about our own *and* other people's responses to what's happening—before, during, and after the conversation.

Once again, think about the beginning of the exchange between Bob and Leslie, when she greets him and asks how the new project is going. When he uses the Observing Participant, Bob can put aside the emotion and look at things more objectively:

> *"I'm reacting strongly because of my past experiences with Leslie. But in this case, I don't really have any data to support this strong reaction. She's just asked a simple question."*

Likewise, Leslie can use her Observing Participant to focus on what may be behind Bob's reaction:

> *"I just meant to ask a friendly question, but Bob seems surprised or irritated. Maybe he thinks I'm checking up on him again."*

This quick assessment of yourself and the other party in the conversation is a prerequisite to the next step in the Observing Participant process: "Exploring" the implications.

How to "Explore"

During the "Explore" step, we mentally connect what's going on right now with the purpose of the interaction. A good mechanical analogy for this stage in the Observing Participant process is the navigation system of an airplane: Once the instruments have read signals from the ground about the plane's exact location, those data are compared to the flight plan to determine whether the plane is on course.

In the Observing Participant process, the "Explore" stage happens when you ask yourself: Will what I sense is going on help or hinder the purpose of this conversation? (This is assuming, of course, that the purpose of the interaction has been clearly determined.) To use our analogy, clarifying the "flight plan" of the conversation is an important part of "Exploring."

Let's return to the conversation between Bob and Leslie. Recall that Bob was using his Observing Participant to exercise some self-control over his strong reaction to Leslie's question. Before he can decide what to say to her, though, he has to make a fundamental decision about what he wants out of this interaction with her. Bob's internal self-talk might sound like this:

> *"I could tell Leslie how I feel about her checking up on me, but maybe I'm jumping to conclusions. I do want to feel that she has confidence in my ability to lead this project."*

Eavesdropping on Leslie's self-talk, we find that she, too, is thinking about what she wants out of the conversation:

> *"I don't want Bob to think I'm prying into his work. I'm just trying to make conversation."*

By considering what's happening in the conversation in light of the purpose each of them has, Bob and Leslie get past their normal stumbling blocks. Thus, the "Explore" stage is a potential turning point in the conversation, based on a clarification of what each person wants in relation to what's happening. In this example, it suits the purposes of both people to take the final step of the "STOP" and "SEE" process: to "Elect" to give a concluding gesture, which will end this brief interaction.

How to "Elect"

To "Elect" means to choose an appropriate communication skill that will help you achieve your purpose. The six communication skills described in Chapter 2 provide you with a number of options. To review:

Choose a **receptive skill** if your purpose will be enhanced by gathering more information and seeking common understanding:

- **Observing**—Continuing to notice what's going on in the interaction

- **Listening**—Active attending to and paraphrasing of what's heard

- **Empathizing**—Understanding and validating the other person's experiences

Choose an **expressive skill** if your purpose will be enhanced by sharing and exchanging information in a direct and constructive manner:

- **Questioning**—Asking for information in a way that gets relevant and appropriately detailed responses

- **Describing**—Giving concrete, objective examples of behavior and its effects

- **Concluding**—Bringing closure to the discussion and making necessary decisions to move on

The choice that you make in taking the "Elect" step moves you from contemplation to action in the conversation. In the case of Bob and Leslie, he might decide to use questioning to clarify the purpose of her inquiry:

"Are you concerned about my work on this project?"

Leslie, on the other hand, might choose to respond by listening and then describing her reasons for selecting Bob to lead the project:

"No, quite the opposite. I asked you to head this particular project because of the expertise you demonstrated on the XYZ project. I'm really very confident in your ability and also very interested in how things are going."

This outcome is clearly different from that of the initial scenario, in which Bob and Leslie were caught up in a cycle of misunderstanding, wasted time and effort, and lack of trust. Use of the Observing Participant not only helped them achieve a successful outcome in this situation but perhaps set the pattern for future performance communication, as well.

▲ Practice, Practice, Practice

The four steps in the Observing Participant "STOP" and "SEE" model—STOP and Sense, Explore, Elect—may seem drawn out and ponderous when each is described separately, as we've done in this chapter. But in practice, we can move through these steps quickly and without missing what's going on in the actual conversation.

The key is *practice*. It takes conscious effort to develop the Observing Participant and regular experience, in a variety of situations, to use it effectively. No doubt, you'll find the Observing Participant easier to use in some situations than others. But as with anything, what seemed impossible the first time gets much easier after several attempts.

An analogy might help you appreciate how to develop your Observing Participant:

Imagine that you've decided to learn how to sail. You spend some time in the classroom, learning terms and what you need to do with the rudder, the ropes, and the sails to guide a vessel in the wind. You learn that in order to reach a point across a lake when going against the wind, you have to make many decisions along the way to implement a tacking maneuver.

After all this thinking and talking, you finally get in a boat and push off. At first, your entire focus is on each discrete step: how to shift the sails, how hard and fast to pull the ropes, how to move the rudder and lean into your turns, and so on. During your first few times out, you may find that while you've honed these discrete skills, you've overshot or failed to reach your planned destination. But as you gain confidence in each move, with each venture, you'll begin to look for where you want to land on the opposite shore.

After a period of time, what initially seemed to be an impossible, complex set of tasks will come much more easily. As a sailor, you'll have realized that you're able to observe the whole process of maneuvering the boat toward a destination while making moment-to-moment decisions and executing appropriate actions.

Similarly, as a partner in a conversation, you can learn to keep track of your purpose and exercise your ability to make the best decisions for reaching it. By engaging your Observing Participant, you can connect what's happening in the conversation with your purpose for having it. Doing so will guide you in making the best possible decisions for selecting skills and achieving On-The-Level communication.

▲ Where Do You Stand?

The Observing Participant, the third basic part of On-The-Level communication, is founded on the first two: the OTL Guiding Principles and Communication Skills. Your understanding of the principles and skills will be put to use in practicing the Observing Participant. And as you gain experience in a variety of performance communication situations, this knowledge and these behaviors will become second nature. You'll *be* an Observing Participant.

Think about your own performance communication practices, as sender and as receiver. Consider the questions that follow, and evaluate where you stand:

- **As a sender, to what extent do you:**

  _____ Listen to your self-talk before, during, and after conversation?

  _____ Pay attention to how the other person is responding to your message, observing nonverbal cues as well as listening to what he or she has to say?

  _____ Step back and consider what you're thinking and feeling, recognizing old patterns of behavior that might get in the way?

  _____ Think about what the other person is thinking and feeling?

  _____ Identify what you want out of the conversation and consider how what's happening might affect attaining it?

  _____ Choose the appropriate communication skill or skills needed to stay on purpose?

  _____ Practice being an Observing Participant, honing your skills with each conversation?

- **As a receiver, to what extent do you:**

  _____ Listen to your self-talk before, during, and after conversation?

  _____ Pay attention to what the sender is telling you, observing nonverbal cues as well as listening to what he or she has to say?

  _____ Step back and consider what you're thinking and feeling, recognizing old patterns of behavior that might get in the way?

  _____ Think about what the sender is thinking and feeling?

_____ Identify what you want out of the conversation and con-sider how what's happening might affect attaining it?

_____ Choose the appropriate communication skill or skills needed to stay on purpose?

_____ Practice being an Observing Participant, honing your skills with each conversation?

Based on your answers, what do you most want to improve about your role as an Observing Participant to make performance communication more On-The-Level?

▲ Key Points

- Effective performance communication involves more than demonstrating proficiency in OTL principles and skills; knowing when to use the skills, in particular, is also essential.

- The Observing Participant will help you stay aware of what's happening in a conversation while it's going on in order to:
  - Think about the purpose of the interaction and then
  - Choose the communication skills that will keep the discussion on track

- The Observing Participant is a type of self-talk that makes you think about the implications of what's going on before, during, and after an important conversation.

- Before a conversation, the Observing Participant helps you formulate a clear purpose and identify how to get started.

- During a conversation, the Observing Participant provides a self-correcting monitor that helps you stay on purpose.

- After a conversation, the Observing Participant guides you to learn from the experience, reviewing what took place and deciding what the most constructive next step might be, if the communication hasn't been completed.

- The "STOP" and "SEE" Model outlines the steps involved in being an Observing Participant. Once you realize a conversation is moving off purpose:

STOP and Sense	Mentally stop yourself for a moment to see what's really going on. Consciously realize what you and the other person are thinking and feeling.
Explore	Think about what you want out of the conversation—your purpose—and how what you're sensing might affect this.
Elect	Given the situation, choose one or more of the six communication skills, and then use them to stay on purpose.

- With practice, your Observing Participant role will come naturally, enabling you to connect what's happening in the conversation with your purpose for having it.

PART II

On-The-Level Communication at Work

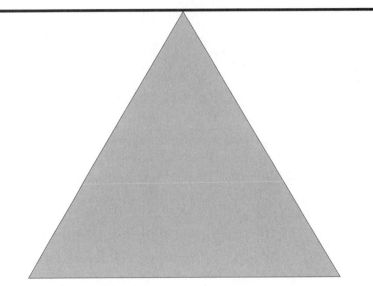

CHAPTER 4

Getting Goal Agreement

In the last quarter of every year since he's been with the company, Bob, a staff accountant, has worked with his key customers and team colleagues to prepare written objectives according to his company's management-by-objectives policy. Typically, however, this has been only a small part of the dynamic goal-setting and -agreement process that Bob's used to become an outstanding performer.

Bob uses On-The-Level communication to get agreement and support regarding his priorities. Whenever he begins a new project, his standard practice is to ask the customer to describe his or her quality requirements. Bob also clarifies who will need to be informed about the progress of the project and what priority it has is in relation to other projects. He makes sure he and key stakeholders have a mutual understanding of what he's expected to achieve or lead. He's the first to renegotiate those expectations when he notices a change in the customer's or organization's priorities or feels that a project needs to be redefined.

Bob doesn't like the wasted effort involved in redoing projects because goals and requirements weren't clearly stated to begin with. He also knows that to be effective, his performance must add value for the customer and support the direction of his company and department. Most importantly, he believes that it's his responsibility to be as clear as possible about what he's expected to contribute. Unlike some of his colleagues, Bob's learned the value of establishing mutually agreed upon goals.

▲ Common Problems

It's difficult to manage others and even yourself when expectations among people who must work together aren't mutually clear. Even when people see the importance of goal agreement, making it happen is often complicated and frustrating. The truth is, many of the systems used to set goals aren't very effective or simply don't work, for a number of reasons:

- *Game Playing*—People often use goals and objectives to set themselves up for budget, performance discussion, and pay decisions. When they do so, their emphasis is on looking good or winning budget battles, rather than on identifying important work. For instance, people may set low goals so they can later exceed them on rating sheets, or they may try to make a job look big so they can justify a higher pay grade. It's difficult to get real goal agreement and commitment among all stakeholders when games like these are being played.

- *Limited Perspective*—Frequently, goals are set in a vacuum, based on personal or team history or on independent ideas about what should be done. When this happens, larger organizational goals and customer needs aren't aggressively explored or incorporated. Setting goals from this limited view sets the stage for customer dissatisfaction and cross-expectations by team members and managers.

- *Vagueness*—Goals may not say enough about the quality requirements that will ensure added value for the customer and success for the business. When goals aren't definitive, the almost inevitable result is that stakeholders have different visions of what the outcomes should be. Teams and individuals, customers and management may think they agree on goals but blissfully march to different drummers until they realize that they disagree about whether a goal has been achieved.

- *Accountability*—Work may proceed with no one truly being accountable for the results. Accountability problems are especially common when teams of people work together to produce complex products or services. Typical comments in such situations include "I don't have the authority," "The other department didn't come through," and "The environment changed." Remarks like these attempt to cover up and excuse a lack of accountability.

- *Incorrect Focus*—Goals may have the wrong focus, defining activities and tasks instead of outputs. The end result—that is, the product or service—is what customers want and is thus the appropriate focus of the goal. Activities and tasks are the means to an end and valuable only if they produce the desired result.

- *Wordiness*—Goal statements may be too wordy, thus obscuring real performance expectations. For instance, they may give more details than necessary, hiding the real message, or they may simply not be well thought through. Wordy goals confuse people and don't communicate expectations that are mutually clear and On-The-Level.

- *Agreement and Ownership*—People often mistake completed goal/objective worksheets for actual agreement and even believe that such documentation provides protection. They feel secure in knowing that they can pull a form out of the file cabinet and say, "See, here are our goals." The fact is, though, that goals really don't exist unless all key stakeholders have agreed to them and taken ownership of them, committing to them as active job priorities.

- *Overkill*—There may be too many goals. When this is the case, tracking and managing them becomes as time consuming as achieving them. Having too many goals also enables individuals and teams to avoid or at least delay difficult prioritization discussions with customers and others. They can put off the tough task of deciding what they will *not* do.

- *Flexibility*—Sometimes, expectations change but goal agreements don't. The result is a conflict between what the individual is asked to contribute and how that contribution is perceived. Goals should be revisited and renegotiated if needed to ensure that they remain relevant, understood, and agreed upon.

- *Impact*—Getting goal agreement may be treated as an intrusion, a formality, or a periodic requirement, nothing more than some paperwork to complete or some deadline to meet. When goal agreement is ignored or made insignificant, goals will have little real impact on performance.

Each of these pitfalls in reaching goal agreement is rooted in the same general problem: a breakdown in communication. In each case, individuals shared inaccurate or incomplete information or denied the importance of face-to-face communication. Sometimes, this happens deliberately; sometimes not. Regardless, when communication breaks down during goal setting, these are the usual results:

- An individual's or team's key priorities don't receive needed budget and other resources. Furthermore, others fail to provide timely support or have cross-expectations because they don't know of or haven't agreed to current priorities.

- Day-to-day pressures, mixed messages, and just plain forgetfulness divert people's energies away from important, planned priorities and toward unplanned, less important issues. During times of crisis, in particular, individuals' responses may be reactive and defensive, not thoughtful and responsible. In these situations, befuddled individuals make sad refrains, such as "But I thought I was supposed to," "I didn't think that was important anymore," and "I didn't have time." And equally unfocused managers or teams scramble to justify the adjustments in budgets and deadlines that inevitably result from having cross-goals.

- Follow-up discussions take a defensive tone and tend to focus on problems and excuses. These discussions, held after the fact, likely cause more anxiety than would have occurred if the desired outputs had been mutually defined and negotiated in the first place. Everyone benefits from agreement about individual and team goals. While it may take time up front to get that agreement, it's usually well worth it, given the time saved in crisis management and rework.

Timing is clearly an important factor in goal agreement. Discussions about goals need to be held at appropriate times, and agreement needs to be reached between relevant parties about performance expectations and priorities. The logical time for such discussions may be at a crucial point in the annual business planning cycle, at the beginning of a new year, at the start of a new project, when organizational priorities change, or when new opportunities or problems arise.

▲ Guidelines for Successful Communication

On-The-Level communication is essential in getting goal agreement. You can avoid the problems discussed earlier by following these OTL guidelines:

1. Find out about the "big picture" context.
2. Get agreement to outputs and roles.
3. Treat goal agreement as an ongoing process.

1. Find Out About the "Big Picture" Context

The "big picture" has two key components: (1) the business's situation and priorities and (2) the customer's needs and expectations. To deal with both, you can take some actions as part of a formal planning process and other actions as needs and opportunities arise. Keep this in mind in considering each component.

The Business's Situation and Priorities

For years, organizations have invented and reinvented planning processes to help them examine their environments, decide what results they want to achieve, and develop priority strategies, programs, and processes. Sometimes, this planning produces useful information to guide the people who do the work, but other times, it doesn't.

Regardless of whether the business's plans are easily accessible and useful for individuals and their teams, it's critical for everyone involved to find out as much as they can about what's important in and around the business and their part of it. You can get this information by talking with people who have broad and inclusive perspectives, including key stakeholders who must ultimately support personal and team goals. Two key questions to ask these people are:

- What key business challenges do we face?
- What do these challenges imply about priorities for our department? for our team? for me?

Reading plans and newsletters will help you answer both questions. But you will get more direct information by being involved either in the planning process itself or in face-to-face dialogue in team or one-on-one meetings. Personal involvement has several important advantages. It helps build support for emerging individual and team goals. In addition, it provides contextual information that serves as a valuable backdrop whenever goal or time-management and trade-off discussions occur.

Direct dialogue between individuals or among team members should be incorporated as a formal part of the planning calendar. For instance, plans may be developed by October, discussed during November, and formalized in December for implementation in the new year. On a more informal basis, "big picture" discussions can occur whenever you have the chance for informal contact with informed people: at lunch, during breaks in meetings, in casual conversations, and so forth.

The Customer's Needs and Expectations

Customers are the people and groups who receive what individuals and teams produce, provide, and deliver. Some customers are **internal.** For example, the people in the manufacturing department are customers of the engineers who design the products the company makes. But everyone in the organization (including external suppliers) must ultimately serve the **external** customers who buy the company's products.

External customers are the reasons organizations and jobs exist; therefore, their needs and expectations are key. Customers today expect their needs and product/service visions to be met, and they feel freer than ever to find alternative suppliers when they're not satisfied. This is becoming true for internal customers, too. They are beginning to buy staff services elsewhere when the internal costs are too high or the value is not satisfactory. In short, it's important to talk with and understand customers and to ensure that goals address their needs.

From another perspective, it's important for customers to talk with and understand their suppliers. Unfortunately, the concern for "customer focus" has unleashed massive amounts of abuse directed against suppliers. Customers should keep in mind that their interests won't be well served if they're not On-The-Level in their relationships with service/product providers. OTL is always a two-way street.

Despite the importance of conversations between suppliers and customers, the fact is, such communication often doesn't occur. Everyone, on both sides—customers and suppliers—makes assumptions. And in the end, people are often disappointed.

It may be impossible to clarify and then meet *all* needs of *all* customers. But suppliers, working as individuals and in teams, can do a number of things to ensure they understand the needs of those they serve:

- Identify key people to contact periodically for a review of products and services. These people may be individual representatives of customer groups or even groups of customers. You might decide to hold a formal meeting with each customer or group, convened specifically to answer questions about your product or service. Or you might address the subject as a side conversation while making another contact.

- In these periodic discussions, ask customers to think about the products and services provided by you or your team. Have them state what they like and don't like, as well as what they need and don't need. Guide this discussion of both positive and negative issues by asking customers what three things they like best and what three things most need improvement. Ask customers how they use what you provide and whether they have additional needs that you could satisfy. Also ask what they get or could get from competitors that you might consider providing.

- If you have a large and diverse customer base, find ways to get formal input and discussion. Focus groups, questionnaires, fax surveys, and phone interviews are options for obtaining this information. Your questions to customers should focus on both expectations and perceptions regarding the quality of products and services as well as the relationship itself.

Customers also play a key role in ensuring that their needs are understood and met. They, too, have specific responsibilities in OTL communication. As a customer, you should:

- Make time to talk with key suppliers, ensuring that your discussions are OTL.

- Think about and relate your needs and requirements to suppliers. Also give them your current assessment of the quality they're providing. When you're not clear about what you want, you can't expect suppliers to guess how best to serve you (unless, of course, you're willing to take whatever you get).

- Talk with suppliers about how you use or intend to use the products or services they provide—for your own needs or for those of your customers. If you withhold information that is vital to supplier understanding and performance, your relationship with them will ultimately suffer.

- Ask suppliers about emerging trends and issues. Listen to their ideas, and respect their expertise and perspective. Be willing to use what you learn from suppliers to help shape your own needs and expectations.

Both receptive and expressive skills are important for creating a mutual understanding of customer needs (see Chapters 2 and 3). Suppliers need to *observe* how their customers use products and services. They must *question* future needs and issues and *listen* to real needs and priorities. Suppliers should be able to accurately *describe* what customers say is important and *conclude* what issues are really pivotal.

Customers need to use OTL skills, as well. They must *observe* their own reactions to products and services and be willing to *describe* and *conclude* what's significant about their needs. Customers must also be willing to learn from their suppliers, *listening* to their observations and opinions and respecting their special expertise.

2. Get Agreement to Outputs and Roles

Goal agreement focuses on two key issues:

1. What outputs will be produced?
2. What roles will occur?

The *output* question requires agreements between individuals/teams and their customers as well as other organization stakeholders (for example, management or affected departments). The *role* question requires agreements among people who need to work together to provide outputs to the customer.

The Output Question

A useful goal has two components:

1. An output statement
2. A list of quality requirements

Outputs are the accomplishments, products, and services (*not the activities*) that individuals or teams are expected to deliver to customers. The outputs that become goals should describe the key accomplishments that individuals or teams will be held accountable for. Here are some sample outputs:

- A design for a specific product
- A new sales process
- A risk analysis for a new venture
- A three-year business plan
- A supplier conference
- Three new marketing reps
- Optimized inventory
- A plant expansion plan
- Implementation of a plant expansion

Output statements should describe what's to be accomplished, not what activities will be needed to accomplish them (unless an activity is required and inflexible; for example, a pilot has to follow a specific safety check procedure before take-off). In addition, output statements should be as specific and concrete as possible so as to avoid confusion about what they mean and when they've been accomplished. For instance, the output "A larger sales force" isn't as specific or clearly stated as "Five new sales reps."

Why should goal agreements focus on outputs rather than activities? The following examples illustrate what may happen when activities, rather than outputs, are stated as goals. First, a family situation:

Mom wants Andy to take care of the lawn and keep it healthy, so she asks him to water it on a regular basis. Andy waters the grass, but in a very cursory way, and he doesn't do anything else. After awhile, the lawn begins to die, causing Mom to rethink her directions to Andy. Does she really want the activity (grass watering), or does she want the output (a healthy lawn)? The latter may mean watering often during a drought or never during a rainy period. Keeping the lawn healthy also may require regular mowing, fertilizing, and eliminating weeds.

Clearly, Mom's directions would've been more effective if she'd stated the output she wanted, not the activity. Given the output—a healthy lawn—Andy would've been accountable for whatever it might take to achieve that.

Now, a business example:

A sales team decides that one of their key goals will be to increase the number of sales calls they make. Maria, a member of the team, asks whether it'll be acceptable for her to make more calls but not necessarily bring in more sales as a result. This prompts some discussion among the team. What they really want is increased sales. When the goal is stated to reflect that output, Maria understands how to go about achieving it: She has to ensure that her sales calls are made to the best prospects and that her approach is high quality. She has to deliver an output, not just complete an activity.

Identifying outputs isn't enough by itself, however. Consider the previous examples again: What's a "healthy lawn"? What constitutes "increased sales"? Individuals may interpret the meanings of these outputs differently, which will further obstruct goal agreement. If goals are to be clear to all stakeholders involved, these individuals must have common expectations regarding what are desirable outputs.

Expectations take the form of **quality requirements** for each output. These are the desired characteristics an output will have when the customer receives it. Quality requirements answer questions such as:

- What quality standards have to be met?
- What quantities have to be provided?
- What deadlines must be met?
- What cost parameters need to be considered?
- Who must be involved?
- What features will delight the customer?

See the table that follows for further examples of outputs and the quality requirements that define them.

Sample Outputs and Quality Requirements

OUTPUT	QUALITY REQUIREMENTS
A home goal: Healthy lawn	• Green • No brown spots • Lawn depth of 3 inches • No weeds
A sales goal: New orders	• Make 5 new calls per week • Secure initial order of over $100 • Secure 80 percent reorder within 30 days • Complete all sales documents and ship to home office within 7 days of sale • Maintain good relations with order-processing staff
An administrative goal: Annual budget	• To be approved by end of the fiscal year • Requires no more than 2 rounds of revisions • Supports key business priorities

- Is flexible enough to encourage creative planning by all groups
- Reduces fixed costs by 10 percent
- Will start all groups with a zero base
- Fosters spirit of teamwork, not competition

An engineer's goal:
Product X design
- Meets needs identified in market study
- Can be produced in existing plant with maximum $50,000 capital investment
- Can be approved for market test by June 30
- Will involve purchasing and manufacturing departments as partners during design stage

An executive goal:
Strategic plan
- Incorporates market and competitive research
- Allows everyone in the organization real opportunity for input
- Defines customer segments, opportunities, and threats
- Identifies key long-term priorities and investments
- Identifies core business competencies
- Will be approved by customer board by August 30

A sales team coordinator's goal:
Launch of new territory
- Achieves projected sales volume of $500,000 in 6 months
- Will be staffed with 6 trained representatives within 3 months
- Includes effective performance communication connection between field and regional staff
- Supported by enthusiastic and positive climate
- Differentiates us from competition among category A and B customers

---

Whether it occurs between suppliers and customers, team members, or suppliers and their own management, any discussion about quality requirements should be creative. Two primary tasks of goal discussions are to sort out priorities and to discuss the costs and benefits of various requirements. All parties should work together to develop the best goal agreement possible.

Customers and suppliers as well as managers must emerge from these discussions with a common vision and commitment. Customers should feel that their needs will be met at the best possible cost. Suppliers should feel that they can provide what customers want within resource constraints. And managers should feel that the strategic direction and positioning of the company will be enhanced by pursuing the goals. Let's consider each entity in turn.

Suppliers   As the supplier, you're the person who owns the goal, so you need to bring all the interests together. Before you attempt to influence customers, have an OTL conversation with yourself. Observe and objectively describe your own assumptions and reactions. Question your own resistance, and deeply examine whether it's possible for you to give customers what they want. Ask yourself these questions:

- Do I really understand my customers' needs and requirements?
- Would they get more value if they changed their requirements?
- What special insights about the product or service do I have and should I share?
- How can I educate customers about my product or service to make them better customers and lead to their greater satisfaction in the long run?

Use the answers to these questions to help you approach the customer. Your first step should be to work with the customer to translate needs into a list of quality requirements. Questioning, listening, and concluding are key OTL skills needed here.

After understanding and stating the customer's requirements, you may want to negotiate expectations, for several reasons. You may disagree, have what you feel is a better idea, or find the costs involved too high. OTL skills will be helpful in these negotiations, too:

- Listen to and empathize with customer needs and requirements. If you show that you understand the customer's needs, he or she will likely be willing to explore alternative routes to getting those needs met.

- Customers often express needs in terms of solutions. Your complete understanding of those needs may stimulate development of another creative solution that you both can support.

- If you feel that certain requirements are impossible or difficult to meet without incurring excessive costs, go back to the need that underlies the requirement and explore other ways of satisfying it. Always show a deep understanding and acceptance of the needs that underlie requests. Empathize with them, describe them, and be ready to explore other ways to address them that represent "wins" for both you and your customer.

- If necessary, educate your customer. As a supplier, you have unique and valuable views regarding solutions and the costs and benefits associated with them. During negotiations with customers, you may need to present these options and analyses. Describing and concluding skills will be valuable. Conversations may include statements like:
  - "You might meet this need in one of several ways, including . . ."
  - "Here are the costs and benefits of each alternative, as I see them . . ."
  - "We could reduce costs by . . ."
  - "For just a small additional investment, we could substantially increase quality in this area . . ."

Giving customers information and choices is a far better alternative than saying no to their requests and expectations. Keep in mind, however, that providing education and addressing choices requires OTL communication that balances receptive and expressive skills.

Your work as a supplier doesn't end with the customer. Often, you need to negotiate with your own management and fellow team members for resources, support, and changed views of products and services. Here, again, OTL skills will be important to your success.

Individuals who work in bureaucratic, hierarchical organizations need their managers' support for agreements with customers as well as their decisions about the amount and scope of work that individuals or teams may accept. Given the nature of bureaucracy, individuals in such organizations may find themselves in the middle of very difficult and conflicting expectations. OTL communication, as illustrated by the following sequence of discussions, can help bring all interests together:

1. Individuals and teams should get as much "big picture" information from management and customers as possible. The discussion with management should begin to identify their broad expectations from the individual or team.

2. Preliminary discussions with customers or their representatives should occur to identify product and service needs and initial quality requirements.

3. Individuals and teams should look at customer expectations in light of current budgets and resources. Before requesting additional resources, individuals and teams should adjust current levels of resources as much as they can without obtaining specific management permission.

4. Individuals and teams should negotiate with their managers to get agreement about what products and services they'll provide and what resources they'll use in doing so. If managers and individuals can't agree about accountabilities, they need to decide what and how to renegotiate with customers. It's imperative that commitments be mutually understood and agreed to by customers, suppliers, and management.

Customers and Management   Customers and management also have OTL responsibilities. Customers should use expressive OTL skills to make their needs and requirements known and receptive OTL skills to find out about issues and alternatives. Managers should adopt a supportive stance toward their staff members and teams, listen to customer needs and resource issues, and support assessing costs and benefits and making trade-offs. In addition, managers should work toward agreements that represent the best value for the customer, a fair return for the organization providing the product or service, and a manageable workload for the personnel involved.

An Example   In order to see the roles of suppliers, customers, and management in action, let's look at an extended example of a service goal expressed as an output with corresponding quality requirements. Note how having an output, rather than an activity, orientation helps everyone concerned support a better customer solution.

Kim Li, hospital director of patient services, was frustrated at the increasing number of complaints received from patients about check-out procedures. In an attempt to solve the problem, she met with Tom, the new team member responsible for implementing checkout procedures. She suggested adding several new checkout procedures and setting more stringent time targets. Tom implemented these suggestions immediately, but the complaints continued. Kim Li's activity-focused management approach wasn't effective in solving the problem.

It finally dawned on Kim Li that she was micromanaging, or focusing too closely on the details of the problem and thus preventing creative thinking about it. She met once again with Tom but tried a new approach. She told him:

"You, Sally, and Pat actually deal with the patients at checkout. I suggest that the three of you meet and figure out what it takes to ensure that we have patient-focused procedures. You still need to cover the minimum paperwork required for insurance purposes, but otherwise, don't be constrained by past practices or existing procedures or assumptions. Checkout procedures are already costly for the hospital; hopefully, your solution will bring down this cost. Talk to patients and other stakeholders, and develop some preliminary quality requirements. Once we agree on those, you and your team can propose a solution."

By stating what she wanted as an output—patient-focused checkouts—Kim Li communicated to Tom in a simple and straightforward way what the service priority needed to be.

After Tom and his team talked with selected patients and other stakeholders (including insurance representatives, nurses, and the hospital administrator), they developed the following quality requirements:

- *Patients are able to go directly home from their rooms.*
- *No information is requested from patients more than once.*
- *The atmosphere is one of friendliness and caring.*
- *Patients have one hospital contact for all administrative matters.*
- *Bills are easy for patients to read and file with other relevant paperwork regarding their hospitalization.*
- *A minimum of recordkeeping is involved for insurance purposes.*
- *Costs are not increased and, if possible, are reduced.*

These quality requirements were agreed on by Kim Li and other key stakeholders. Given that approval, Tom's team, free of the mandate to take specific actions, began to propose ways to meet the quality requirements. Ultimately, changes were implemented in admissions processes, information and data-processing practices, and actual checkout procedures.

As this example shows, stating goals in terms of outputs and quality requirements is essential in reaching goal agreement, for several reasons. When outputs and quality requirements are stated, a vision is created that all stakeholders can adopt. And given this foundation, the individuals and teams who have to accomplish the goals can be creative and flexible in designing the performance actions to take.

The Role Question

Most work today requires collaboration and broad support from people outside the team, including external suppliers and even customers themselves. Involvement of this level creates several problems and increases the need for really effective performance communication. All stakeholders involved must agree both to the goal and its quality requirements and to the roles they'll play in accomplishing it.

Here are some tips for ensuring active agreement:

- In describing the output and quality requirements, involve everyone who must work together on the goal. Doing this may require bringing people together from other work units, a practice that may be unusual in your organization. Most goal-setting processes today are still built around organization charts (which are departmentalized), rather than natural work teams (which are often cross-functional). Goal discussions shouldn't be constrained by formal structures.

- Identify a leader for every team goal. The leader will be responsible for keeping the quality requirements up to date, coordinating the work and resources, and ensuring that customers, management, and team members are involved. The leader may be a volunteer team member, someone designated by management, or someone selected by the team.

- Identify those people who will provide support and ensure that roles have been defined as clearly as possible (for example, customer contact, work responsibilities, communication within the team or with you).

- Get agreement regarding outputs and quality requirements from the people who provide budget and other resources. Don't assume that resources will be provided automatically. Have face-to-face discussions about the time, people, technology, and budgets involved in reaching goals.

- Reach agreement about what you will *not* do if priorities shift. Don't fall into the trap of adding major new work to an already full plate. Use goal-agreement discussions as opportunities to talk about what you may stop doing as well as what you want to initiate or change.

In this era of self-management and empowerment, individuals should develop their own goals, rather than expect management to do so. The role of management should be to ensure that the "big picture" is communicated and discussed, that customers are involved in performance communication, and that resource and priority trade-offs support the organization's larger needs. Individuals and teams shouldn't perpetuate the myth that management's role is to tell people what their jobs are. Self-management and empowerment can work to everyone's advantage through the use of OTL communication.

3. Treat Goal Agreement as an Ongoing Process

For many people, goals have little credibility. Why? Some individuals have a generally reactive approach to work and life, so planning is irrelevant. Others have had too many experiences in which goals have been interrupted or forgotten, and still others have been frustrated by shifting or unclear business priorities. And some people feel they've been overmanaged and have little autonomy; they just follow orders and whims.

The purpose of goal setting is complicated in today's rapidly changing environment. On the one hand, organizations and people need goals to remain focused, to allocate resources, and to evaluate results. On the other hand, setting and adhering to inflexible goals can prevent opportunism and may keep people on paths to failure.

Goals should be considered as means to alignment, personal focus, and sanity. Performance goals are agreements between customers and performers and between performers and managers/team members. At their best, performance goals identify important outputs that wouldn't be achieved under normal day-to-day pressures or in the midst of crises. For instance, sales reps who are busy servicing their regular customers may intend to make new contacts but never get around to it, or they may do so sporadically, as opportunities arise. Setting the individual goal "Expand new customer base" will help ensure that outcomes like this, which require a break from normal work patterns, will occur.

It follows that work on performance goals will often conflict with other events and ideas, both day-to-day tasks and issues that seem important at the moment. The sales rep, for instance, may find it difficult to make five new calls during the week he or she is expected to cover for a vacationing co-worker. Likewise, making new calls may seem less important during a crisis, such as a quality-control problem that draws complaints from a large number of customers.

In instances like these, performance goals must be defended against short-term requirements and events. The same is true of spur-of-the-moment initiatives, such as changes in company policies or operations. Sometimes these ad hoc events and ideas are important enough to drive changes in priorities; other times, they're not. The point to remember is that when changing environments or circumstances conflicts with performance goals, OTL communication must occur.

Performance goals should be considered as the "home base" for performance communication. When these goals are in jeopardy, customers and other stakeholders should be approached to confirm commitments and resources or to renegotiate new priorities. If a customer, manager, or team member adds expectations without eliminating or revising others, think creatively about how you can respond. If you feel the new expectations threaten existing commitments to goals, let the other stakeholders know about it. Perhaps priorities can be renegotiated and new goals put in place. The most common response is to take on additional short-term responsibilities and let other commitments slip. Slippage is okay only if the priorities have really changed and key stakeholders are aware of the consequences.

The following conversation between a manager, Ellen, and customer service representative, Jean, illustrates effective OTL communication in which goal agreement is an ongoing process:

> Ellen: *"I have an idea that I'd like you to work on, Jean. I think we need to get some new technology in here to help us keep track of and analyze the kinds of questions customers are raising. Would you find out what's available and make a recommendation? I'd like it within the next few weeks."*

Jean: *"Let's take some time clarifying the quality requirements. I'll need to talk with you further, as well as with anyone else who'll use the data. I also want to figure out the time and costs involved. As you know, I'm working on two other big projects in addition to my normal customer contact activities. If I do this, I'll probably have to change*  *some of my goals or get other people involved. I'll set up an appointment with you for next week, Ellen, and we can discuss some of these issues then."*

A frequent response in situations like this—especially when the boss asks for work to be done—is to agree to the request without thinking about what it involves and what effect it'll have on other priorities. In her response, Jean acknowledges Ellen's request but doesn't arbitrarily agree to it. Instead, Jean raises a number of relevant issues, including the need for more information, and suggests a future meeting to follow up. She's given herself the opportunity to make a recommendation based on all available information, ensuring that her proposal will be realistic and well thought out. This won't only benefit Jean but her manager and the company, too.

In her next meeting with Ellen, Jean's able to respond with confidence:

"Ellen, I've looked into your request. In addition to talking with you, I've talked with the others we agreed will be customers. Everyone thinks the work is worth doing. In fact, given our business strategy, it's probably more important than the other two

projects I'm working on. But I can't do all three. I suggest we extend the timeline on project A; give me another two months on it. As for project B, I've talked with Dan, and he's willing to take it on. What do you think?"

This dialogue between Ellen and Jean is the type of OTL conversation that *should* occur frequently but rarely does. Too often, goal agreement is either eliminated entirely or done in a cursory way. The ultimate result is unguided or misdirected work.

Goals should be rallying points for discussion. They can ensure that resources are always used well. They can keep an organization and its members focused. They can make sure that important work actually gets done. Of course, none of these things happens without continuous and sometimes tough discussions about priorities.

In an OTL environment, written goals are both as stable as possible and as dynamic as necessary to meet customer and business needs and to support individual direction and sanity. It's not unusual to revise goals: adding new outputs, changing quality requirements, deleting outputs, and so on. While revision may wreak havoc with written goals, this inconvenience shouldn't stand in the way of reevaluating and reprioritizing goals, when this is needed.

Goal agreement is a key success factor in high-quality performance. Goals both support and are supported by performance communication that's direct, respectful and purposeful and that involves shared responsibility—in other words, On-The-Level.

▲ Where Do You Stand?

In some ways, this emphasis on performance communication regarding goals is a new one. Examining how they communicate is a unique and challenging experience for many people. But the fact is, all other aspects of work—flexibility, focus, alignment, use of resources, team synergy, and personal fulfillment—depend on performance communication. How successful that communication will be depends on the people involved.

Success depends on everyone playing an active role to clarify the "big picture" context; to agree to outputs, quality requirements, and roles; and to ensure ongoing agreement. Deliberate, On-The-Level communication about performance goals is the joint responsibility of all stakeholders.

Think about your own goal-agreement practices, as a supplier, customer, or manager. Consider the questions that follow, and evaluate where you stand:

- **As a supplier (whether individual or team member), to what extent do you:**

    ____ Find out about the "big picture" regarding the business's priorities and the customer's needs?

    ____ Negotiate outputs, not activities, and get agreement to quality requirements?

    ____ Communicate to get agreement about what you will *not* do as well as what you *will* do?

    ____ Make sure the people who need to support you agree to the roles stated in your goals?

    ____ Use goals to help make trade-offs regarding your own time management?

    ____ Stay flexible in accepting new work yet raise issues, make changes, or take a stand when goals are in jeopardy?

- **As a customer, to what extent do you:**

    ____ Clarify your real needs and communicate them willingly to suppliers?

    ____ Help your suppliers create visions for their products or services by being clear about your quality requirements?

    ____ Treat your suppliers as partners, listening to them and working toward optimal agreements?

    ____ Communicate when your requirements change or when you have information that will affect goals?

- **As a manager, to what extent do you:**

  ____ Help people in your organization understand the larger priorities of the business and department, involving them in planning and strategy development, if possible?

  ____ Support customer contact and the role of the customer in deciding outputs and quality requirements?

  ____ Support individual and team goal setting by refusing to dictate goals, instead responding to and shaping others' goal ideas?

  ____ Ensure that your own expectations are clear and focused on benefits for customers, rather than on your need to control or meet arbitrary bureaucratic requirements?

  ____ Expect people to use their goals and to defend them when challenged by more compelling but less important work?

  ____ Support flexibility and change whenever required but always keep the "big picture" in mind, reminding people of it when necessary?

Based on your answers, what do you most want to improve about your role in goal agreement to make it more On-The-Level?

▲ Key Points

- Goal agreement is a key success factor in high-quality performance.

- Goal agreement ensures alignment among all stakeholders (customers, suppliers, and managers) as well as personal focus and sanity.

- Even when the importance of goal agreement is recognized, trying to achieve it may be complicated and frustrating because many of the systems used to set goals aren't very effective or simply don't work.

- Today more than ever, communicating On-The-Level is vital to getting goal agreement. Performance goals should be the "home base" for performance communication.

- Three OTL guidelines will ensure getting goal agreement:
  - Find out about the "big picture" context.
  - Get agreement to outputs and roles.
  - Treat goal agreement as an ongoing process.

- Suppliers, customers, and managers must understand their unique roles and responsibilities in getting goal agreement.

CHAPTER 5

Giving and Receiving Feedback

The 18 months Lin was in the marketing department were hectic. She had to learn a lot in a very short period of time, and she received very little encouragement or other feedback from her manager, Douglas. Given this lack of feedback, Lin developed what she felt was an effective strategy for knowing where she stood with Douglas by interpreting the hidden meanings she found in his comments and actions. For instance, she watched how he assigned projects and noted when he invited her to some meetings but not others. Overall, their work together went well, but Lin eventually concluded that Douglas didn't think much of her performance. She decided to move on and quickly found a job with another company.

Lin's resignation and the reasons she cited for leaving caught Douglas off guard. In response, he said he'd always thought that her work was outstanding and that she had a bright future in marketing management, opinions he'd shared with a number of colleagues. Upon hearing such

positive remarks, Lin was surprised and confused; she had no idea Douglas felt that way.

Her mind made up, Lin left the company feeling unappreciated; she had worked hard, and it had gotten her nowhere. Douglas felt taken advantage of, as if Lin had used him and the company as a training ground. How could these two people have gotten so far off track?

▲ Common Problems

Analyses of human communication are full of terms taken from other fields in order to create useful analogies. The term *feedback,* for instance, was originally an engineering term. According to *Webster's, feedback* is "the return to the input of a part of the output of a machine, system or process." In other words, part of what's been produced is returned to ("fed back to") the beginning of the production process in order to evaluate or correct the process. The *output* becomes the *input* for the next action.

Using the term in the context of communication, **feedback** can likewise be thought of as a process: observing an action or system and gathering information about it for the purpose of evaluation or correction. In a more general sense, *Webster's* defines feedback as "the information so transmitted," which makes it something tangible, as well.

The latter is probably close to the definition that most of us hold, even though we've probably never put it into words. The fact is, we've been giving and receiving feedback our entire lives, beginning with some of our earliest interactions as children. For most of us, however, this lifetime of experience as senders and receivers hasn't helped us understand let alone be comfortable with feedback.

For instance, when someone who's important to us says "I have some feedback for you," our anxiety level rises and we feel our defense shields start to go up. We expect the worst. Some of the same emotions enter in when we're on the other side of the exchange, preparing to give feedback to someone we think is going to react defensively. We might wonder if what we have to say is even worth bringing up, given the response it might bring.

So what are we doing wrong? People giving feedback, or **senders,** commonly make these mistakes:

- *Vagueness*—Senders usually think they're clear and specific about the content and purpose of their feedback. But when they translate their message into words, it often comes out as a vague generalization. Receivers will understandably have a hard time interpreting the message and, in frustration, may react defensively.

- *Shutting Down*—Senders who are anxious about giving feedback may feel that once they've stated their message, they've finished communicating. Doing so has the effect of cutting off communication after feedback has been received, instead of encouraging dialogue about it. Receivers may feel denied the opportunity to respond, which, once again, will prompt a defensive reaction.

- *Anticipation*—Senders often think they know how the people receiving feedback will respond, so they try to anticipate those reactions, perhaps even planning measures to address them. As a result, senders spend more energy trying to take care of the feelings of the receivers than they do focusing on the clarity of the information they want to send. Receivers may find this patronizing and manipulative.

Receivers of feedback are equally prone to certain pitfalls:

- *Expecting the Worst*—When they suspect feedback is coming, receivers often assume that what they're about to hear is a criticism and, as a result, start to get defensive. This is unfair to senders, who haven't yet delivered their message. Moreover, faced with this defensive attitude from receivers, senders may get defensive themselves, preparing for conflict.

- *Counterattacking*—When receivers get feedback they don't like, they sometimes counterattack by returning messages of equal weight to the senders. The original message is ultimately lost because the receivers don't listen or try to understand it. Senders may feel their communication has been futile and will likely resent the counterattack. Once more, defensive shields will go up on both sides.

- *Passiveness*—Receivers sometimes see their role as a passive one, assuming that senders are in charge of the feedback communication. By making this assumption, receivers limit their full participation and completely overlook the possibility of actively *seeking* feedback. Senders may become more anxious if they feel they have to carry the whole burden of responsibility for communicating feedback.

At one time, people only thought of feedback as something managers gave to staff members about their performance. The notion that managers also need to *receive* feedback from the people they lead wasn't even considered, nor were exchanges of feedback between co-workers or customers and suppliers.

These beliefs have changed in recent years due to the increased focus on teams and the need to work across functional boundaries. Managers often find themselves without opportunities to directly observe the performance of their staff members; to get the information needed, others need to be involved in performance discussions. In these instances, staff need support and coaching from their managers on how to give feedback directly to the peers they work with most closely. Peers, suppliers, and customers, in particular, are potentially positioned to give useful feedback to one another. Some organizations refer to this as *360 degree feedback*. Whatever it's called, feedback today—and for the future—must come from multiple and relevant sources.

▲ Guidelines for Successful Communication

Before discussing guidelines for giving and receiving feedback, it'll be helpful to review the Guiding Principles of On-The-Level communication, both in general terms and in the specific context of feedback communication, whatever the source:

- *Directness—Stating honestly and openly what you know, think, feel, or need.* Feedback should be specific and timely, and parties on both sides should express themselves openly. They should do their best to avoid communication games that force messages underground, creating confusion and anxiety for both senders and receivers. (See the section on "Communication Games" in Chapter 2.)

- *Respect—Treating others with dignity and consideration for their thoughts, feelings, and opinions.* Communication that attacks or counterattacks isn't respectful. Effective feedback allows information to be shared without blaming or judging. It facilitates the development of understanding and consideration between the parties involved and prevents any attempts they might make to diminish one another.

- *Shared responsibility—Ensuring two-way communication that focuses on achieving positive, mutually satisfying results.* Everyone has a role in creating open communication about performance results and about enhancing skills and work styles. Senders aren't exclusively responsible for initiating feedback nor are receivers limited to being passive and subordinate.

- *Purpose—Identifying what you want to accomplish in the discussion and adjusting actions and words as needed to reach the desired outcomes.* Feedback needs to be delivered with a clear focus in mind, a purpose in terms of creating or improving results and developing skills. When that purpose is clear, the message will likely be heard and acted on. Feedback that intends to vent anger or hurt is misdirected (as well as irresponsible).

Following the four OTL principles should give you confidence in all feedback exchanges: between managers and staff members, between colleagues, across functional lines, and between suppliers and customers. Nonetheless, as a sender, you may still feel a bit reluctant to be direct. It's possible to be too confrontational. If you cross that line, you'll likely be met with a defensive reaction. It's equally possible, however, to try too hard to take care of the receiver's feelings and risk diminishing the clarity of your message.

The figure that follows illustrates what may at times appear to be cross-purposes in delivering feedback: being direct (the horizontal axis) and showing respect for feelings (the vertical axis). Arrow A shows that when strong respect for feelings occurs at the expense of being direct, it effectively buries the message. Arrow C shows that focusing exclusively on directness, without respecting feelings, risks getting a defensive reaction, which can shut down communication. Arrow B represents a healthy concern for both purposes and thus effective OTL feedback communication.

To help ensure that you achieve this balance between directness and concern for feelings, apply the OTL Communication Skills: The receptive skills will help you show appropriate concern for feelings, and the expressive skills will help you express information and positions directly.

Cross-Purposes in Delivering Feedback

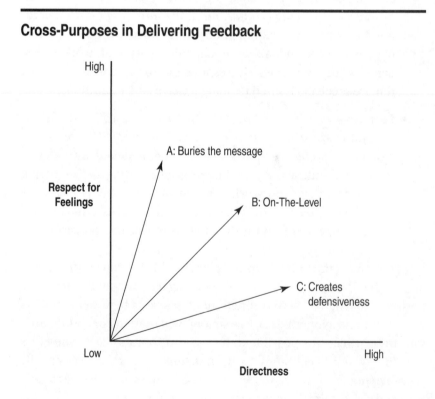

In addition to applying the OTL principles and communication skills, these six guidelines will help you achieve effective feedback communication:

1. Think of feedback as information.
2. Organize your thoughts before giving feedback.
3. Ask for feedback.
4. Use a listening template when receiving feedback.
5. Keep the human element.
6. Focus on outputs, competencies, and style.

1. Think of Feedback as Information

Earlier in the chapter, we defined *feedback* as both an ongoing exchange of information (a process) and the information exchanged (a product). Thinking of feedback as something tangible—as information—makes it something we can work with. For many people, holding this viewpoint takes away some of the emotion of exchanging feedback, which is a big first step in achieving OTL communication.

Feedback, as information, can be classified as *inputs* and *outputs:* information fed into and received from the communication process, which is ongoing. A thermostat is a good example of this concept. Based on a reading of the current temperature in a room in relation to a preset desired temperature (information), the thermostat will signal the furnace to turn on or off. If the current reading is lower than the desired temperature, for instance, the thermostat will signal the furnace to turn on. The output of the furnace will be heat, which will raise the temperature in the room until it reaches the desired temperature (information). At that point, the thermostat will signal the furnace to shut off. This cycle will operate continuously to maintain the desired temperature.

This thermostat analogy for communication breaks down when we consider the intellectual and emotional reactions people have to information. The thermostat doesn't think about the information it receives or what role it plays, and the furnace doesn't feel hurt when it's told to shut off or appreciated when it's told to turn on.

Nevertheless, the analogy raises a useful question: What if we *could* look at feedback as information? This isn't to say that we wouldn't have reactions, emotional or intellectual—that expectation would be unrealistic. Rather, it suggests that if we could separate our reactions from the information itself, we would be more inclined to explore and understand the message.

Let's consider an example from the world of work:

Mark, a finance manager working on a cross-functional team with Carmen, an engineer, censored himself from giving feedback about her individualistic way of working.

Even though he had a clear, direct message that might have given Carmen some insight into the effect of her working style on others, Mark decided that it wasn't his job to assess some-one who didn't directly re-port to him. Carmen's engi-neering manager was respon-sible for giving her performance feedback, but because her manager didn't have firsthand observations of Carmen's working style, the information wasn't passed on. As a result, Carmen didn't get feedback that may have helped her and oth-ers working with her.

This situation might have gone differently if Mark, the finance manager, had thought, "If I share this information with Carmen, *she* can assess whether it's useful." Mark didn't have to play the *assessor* role, only the *communicator* role. If he had thought of feed-back as information and could have communicated it as such to Car-men, this might have been a significant coaching and learning op-portunity.

In evaluating individuals' performance, managers, team members, and customers may have to give both information and assessments for performance feedback discussions. In most companies, the annual performance discussion is the primary vehicle for performance feedback. Feedback is boiled down to ratings, or numbers, which influence compensation decisions and can often affect promotion. This focus is unfortunate because the numbers overshadow other descriptive information in the feedback. Many managers split the focus of performance discussions to make sure that information about improvement, appreciation, and development is really discussed and heard.

The individual receiving feedback can also separate performance discussion ratings from specific observations and conclusions made by people giving feedback. When ratings are received in a performance feedback discussion, the individual should ask to see the information the numbers are based on and to discuss those details. After that, if the individual realizes that emotional reactions blocked his or her ability to explore the information the ratings were based on, then he or she should ask for a follow-up discussion to better understand the feedback.

Senders of feedback should keep in mind that they're communicating for a *purpose* and focus on the skills of describing and concluding. Receivers of feedback should remind themselves that useful information is being presented, even if their initial reaction to hearing it is defensive. Concentrating on the information itself will help both sides of the feedback exchange get around emotional and intellectual defenses.

2. Organize Your Thoughts Before Giving Feedback

Giving and receiving feedback can be frustrating when the moment presents itself to discuss an issue and the words all come out in a jumble. If the person sending the feedback hasn't organized his or her thoughts, the message and how it's delivered will be difficult to follow. Feedback communication can be enhanced when it's given some structure.

When you're mentally preparing to give feedback, try to answer these questions:

1. *What have I observed that makes me want to give feedback?* In your mind, describe your observations, but don't draw any conclusions; that is, gather objective details without making subjective judgments. This will help you focus on what aspect of an issue you want to raise. If you can't focus specifically, the issue isn't yet clear to you, which means you won't be able to express yourself clearly to anyone else.

   For example, suppose you're a store manager and observe Ron, a sales associate, approach a customer and tell her what she needs before she has a chance to explain. In preparing to give feedback to Ron, think carefully about what you observed, concentrating on the details of the exchange: who said what? to whom? when? and so on. Remember that observations provide concrete examples, which are part of the describing activities in a discussion.

2. *Why are the observations I have described important?* In this step, you want to describe the results or effects of the behavior. As you consider how to express the importance of the example, try to pinpoint what about it will matter to the receiver. Answer the question "So what?" from the receiver's point of view, as much as possible.

   As the store manager, ask and answer two questions: (a) What's important about the observation you made of Ron? If Ron's premature assumption about what a customer wants is wrong, he'll probably not make the sale. Even if he does, the customer will leave feeling unheard and perhaps taken advantage of. If Ron understands the customer's needs, he can respond to them accurately, which will please the customer and likely close the sale. (b) Why should this matter to Ron? If customers' needs are met, they'll come back. Ron will enjoy increased sales and may even develop a regular clientele, both of which will reflect favorably on him.

3. *What do I want to happen?* Use concluding skills to deduce implications and propose ideas about what different results might be achieved and how. This step is most effective when the ideas about what to do come from the person receiving the feedback. But brainstorming now, in preparing for that feedback, will help you be clear about what you really want to happen.

As the store manager, what do you want to happen? Increased sales and development of regular clientele. How can you achieve this? Through improving the service of your sales associates—in this case, Ron. More specifically, you could suggest that when he greets new customers, Ron should spend the first few minutes asking them questions about their needs. Involve Ron in determining what kinds of questions would get the most information.

A short-hand reference for this three-part structure is **observation–importance–want.** It works in preparing to give positive feedback as well as feedback calling for constructive change. This approach is appropriate for managers, staff members, co-workers, and customers who are delivering feedback about performance results or individual skills or style.

When actually communicating your feedback, it's more important to discuss all three questions than to answer them in sequence. Your message should include the three components mentioned: the *observations,* the *importance* statement, and the *want* statement. But the order in which you present them can be flexible. You should decide what's appropriate for the situation at hand.

If you have difficulty organizing your thoughts or are anxious about presenting your feedback, use the three-part structure both in preparation and delivery. The *observations* will force you to anchor your feedback in specific past events, the *importance* question will bring the issue into the present, and the *want* component will address the future. When these three pieces of the feedback message are clear in your mind, you'll be able to talk about them easily.

If the feedback situation is an especially important one and you have ample time to really think about and prepare what to say, find a friend who'll listen to a "dry run" of your feedback. Ask your listener to look for the following:

- Are the *observations* really descriptions of examples, or are they generalizations and judgments?
- Does the *importance* statement address an effect the receiver cares about?
- Does the *want* element provide specific suggestions or allow for problem solving?

In addition, ask your listener to give his or her general reactions to your feedback, in terms of the message itself and how it's delivered. This process of structuring your thoughts will help clarify the focus of your feedback and will raise your self-confidence about delivering the message. The receiver will benefit, as well, because your message will be clear and easy to follow.

3. Ask for Feedback

When the idea of encouraging feedback is discussed in most organizations, the emphasis is on *giving* feedback. Managers, for example, are often trained to give better feedback in performance and coaching discussions, and team members are encouraged to give feedback to their peers in order to improve team functioning. But what about those who *receive* feedback? What can they do to help the feedback process?

The single most effective action receivers can take is to *ask* for feedback. An invitation for feedback helps communication in three ways:

1. It helps the sender know that the receiver is ready to hear feedback and is perhaps relatively nondefensive.
2. Depending on how specific the request for feedback is, the sender can focus his or her observations and conclusions accordingly.
3. Asking for feedback models the shared responsibility senders and receivers have for OTL feedback communication.

Most of us know from experience that it's far easier to give feedback to someone who's asked for it than to someone who hasn't. But getting people to ask for feedback can present a real challenge. Everyone may need encouragement.

Once the exchange has begun, though, the results can often be felt immediately. For instance, a team that asks for specific feedback on a project will get the exact information they need in a timely way. Performance will be improved, and communication will be made less stressful.

Regardless of whether your organization encourages asking for feedback, you can create a norm for doing so in your immediate work group. At first, people may not be comfortable giving honest, direct responses because they may not be sure that your request for feedback is genuine. When this is the case, people will give you safe responses, telling you what they think you want to hear. Managers asking staff members for feedback often experience this phenomenon. When you ask people for feedback, you may also catch them off guard. They may be hesitant or unable at that moment to put their observations and conclusions into words.

Follow these suggestions when asking for feedback:

1. *Make your request specific.* If your request for information is vague, the response you receive will likely be vague, too. A general question, such as "Do you have any feedback for me?" will probably draw a response like "No, I think everything is fine." A specific question, on the other hand, will increase the credibility of the request and will more likely get a thoughtful, specific response. For instance, the following questions ask for specific information and communicate an authentic interest in feedback: "We had our first project meeting today. What important information did you get from it? What do you think we can do to make the next meeting better for you?"

2. *Ask for information, not an assessment.* As you begin to experiment with asking for feedback, keep in mind that the people you're asking may feel threatened if your requests call for evaluation. Staff members who are asked for feedback from their

managers may be particularly sensitive. A request such as "So, tell me how I am doing" will generally get a response like "You're doing great!" One way to shift the emphasis away from assessment and focus on information is to follow the request for evaluative feedback with questions such as these:

– "What would you like to see more of?"
– "What would you like to see less of?"
– "What would you like to see kept the same?"

By following up your own general question with specific questions, you'll steer the other person to give examples of real behaviors and events, rather than simply stating whether things are generally good or bad.

3. *Give people time to prepare feedback for you.* Few of us would feel confident giving constructive feedback immediately in response to an unexpected request. Rather than put people on the spot like this, give them advanced notice that you'll be asking for feedback, or make your request and ask people to get back to you. Allowing people time to prepare feedback is considerate and professional; doing so will also help ensure that the information you receive is accurate and thorough.

4. *Be persistent about requesting feedback.* If your first few attempts at asking for feedback don't get substantive responses, don't give up. Initially, people may be unsure whether your request is genuine, especially if asking for feedback isn't normally done in your organization. Being persistent about asking is one way of demonstrating that you really do want feedback from others.

Unfortunately, many people believe that asking for feedback is a sign of weakness. They think that competent people don't need help and that asking for feedback is somehow an admission of being unable to perform independently. This view ignores the fact that people need information to learn. It also denies that people sometimes have on "blinders" and, for whatever reason, don't see things from all relevant points of view.

4. Use a Listening Template When Receiving Feedback

The structure that was provided earlier for organizing and delivering feedback is also a useful template for *receiving* feedback. When you know someone is trying to give you feedback and you aren't clear about the message, you can improve the focus of the discussion by actively seeking the other person's *observations*, his or her view of the *importance* of those observations, and the outcomes he or she *wants* to achieve.

In addition to helping you organize the information presented, this three-part structure can help you concentrate on understanding the feedback. Breaking something into parts or steps and looking at each separately is often a useful means of understanding the whole. In terms of receiving feedback, following this approach will ensure that you understand the message accurately and completely before you respond to it.

By asking a number of probing questions, you'll be able to listen actively to feedback:

- To get more information about *observations*, ask:
  - "What example of the problem can you give me?"
  - "When did you first notice this happening?"
  - "In what kinds of situations have you observed this happening?"

- To get more information about *importance*, ask:
  - "Help me understand how you experienced the situation. What effect did it have on you?"
  - "How do you see this impacting our goals, the project, and so on?"
  - "You're obviously concerned. Can you tell me more about why this is important to you?"

- To get more information about *wants*, ask:
  - "What could've been done differently to improve the situation?"
  - "What would it take to have a more positive effect?"
  - "What ideas do you have for achieving a better result?"

By asking questions like these, the person receiving feedback takes an active role in focusing the message. Doing so helps the receiver understand the message and may also help the sender organize and clarify what he or she wants to say. Asking these types of questions also keeps the conversation focused on outcomes rather than on blame and defensiveness.

5. Keep the Human Element

Feedback communication occurs between two human beings. This means that it's always a partially subjective process, one that can't be mechanized or replaced by forms or computers. Acknowledging the human element, feedback is most meaningful when the exchange is face to face or voice to voice and rooted in a personal commitment to being On-The-Level.

Organizations that want to encourage feedback from multiple sources can initiate the process by using anonymous feedback forms. They provide the opportunity to share information but without specifying from whom. This consolidated feedback provides general results. Once people have had some experience giving and receiving feedback in this way, they can work toward complete face-to-face, voice-to-voice feedback.

Work teams in the early stages may also have difficulty exchanging feedback. The trust level may not allow for open, candid feedback discussions, and there's a learning curve for handling such discussions effectively. Eventually, however, the team will need to talk about results. A written survey may be used initially to get specific information from team members, but the exchange shouldn't stop there. Members must also follow up and discuss the information, not just take results at face value from the form. The ultimate goal is to make OTL feedback a normal part of team operation. It needs to be a human process, not a mechanical one.

Keeping the human element is even more difficult during a performance feedback discussion, in which the manager or team must both give feedback and assess performance. Certainly, it's important to be as objective as possible when trying to describe and assess performance. It's also essential to recognize and stop communication games when they occur. But these efforts will be only as effective as the level of trust that exists between the manager or team and the individual.

Trust can be nurtured by talking openly about concerns, opinions, and reactions. The more information people have about what you've observed and why those observations are important to you, the more they'll trust your conclusions. In most cases, if you're willing to talk about not just your conclusions but the observations, thoughts, values, and feelings behind them, then the other person will be likely to talk openly, as well. Think of this process as communicating the *why* behind the *what* of your communication.

If you're the person giving feedback, or the sender, consider these suggestions for keeping the human element in your communication:

- Talk with staff members or team members about how performance discussions and appraisals are currently done: Are outputs, competency, and style discussed openly and directly? Are performance discussions just assignments of ratings or numbers, or is specific information shared and discussed? After getting and organizing this input, describe what specific actions you'll take to improve performance discussions and help people feel comfortable with them. Then act on your commitments. Communicate that you want performance discussions to be On-The-Level.

- In considering the *importance* aspect of the feedback message, remember to ask "So what?": that is, what about the situation should be important to the person receiving the feedback? Doing so employs the skill of *empathy,* or seeing things from another person's point of view. In terms of giving feedback, this means determining what's important according to the receiver's values and interests, not your own. Although it may not be possible to completely understand another person's viewpoint, the receiver will appreciate your effort.

- During any feedback exchange, if it feels as though you're just going through the motions, rather than having a productive discussion, stop and ask what would improve the exchange. Don't expect feedback communication to be perfect or to proceed according to some grand design. Do expect the skills you bring to feedback discussions to improve steadily with use. If either you or the receiver get off track or slip into a game, acknowledge it and move on to improve the discussion.

If you're receiving feedback, you can also act to improve the human quality of communication:

- Discuss your experiences in performance discussions with your manager or co-workers: Are the discussions open and candid? Do you receive sufficiently detailed information to understand the quality of your performance? Is performance communication a two-way process? By bringing your concerns about performance feedback to the individuals who will act on any conclusions drawn from the discussion, you demonstrate your commitment to the feedback process. In response, the person giving the feedback will probably appreciate your input and take your suggestions to heart.

- When you receive feedback, try to *respond,* not *react.* In other words, try to separate the emotion from the message. If you can't immediately absorb the information delivered and respond to it effectively, buy some time. Listen as best you can, and then ask the person giving the feedback to continue the discussion later. Explain that you'd like to consider the information and prepare an appropriate response. Taking this approach doesn't mean denying your emotions. It means acknowledging that they may interfere with effective communication. If you're comfortable telling the sender that you feel overwhelmed or upset by the feedback, do so. But as much as possible, remain calm and tactful.

- If you have sufficient notice of a feedback discussion, think about how the sender will approach it, particularly in terms of the *importance* and *want* issues. Considering the interests of others, and not just your own, may give you an important reality check. What's more, your show of empathy will likely be appreciated by the sender. Be very careful, though, that you don't make unwarranted assumptions about what feedback you expect or the person who'll deliver it. Don't go into the discussion ready to do battle.

- Don't let the person giving the feedback do all the work. If a discussion isn't meaningful, talk about why and what would help. And if feedback isn't forthcoming, ask for it with a specific purpose in mind. As with all OTL communication, feedback should be a two-way exchange.

6. Focus on Outputs, Competencies, and Style

This guideline is directed specifically to performance feedback—situations in which managers, project leaders, and team leaders are responsible for assessing performance as well as making suggestions on skill development to enhance performance.

Evaluating and discussing performance is complicated because what individuals do from day to day has both *short- and long-term implications.* So for performance feedback to be thorough and meaningful, it should address not only what an individual has accomplished in the short term. It should also look at how those accomplishments were achieved and what long-term impact they have had or may have on others inside and outside the organization. Looking at these implications involves discussing the knowledge and skills the person used or should have used in situations where his or her competencies were key factors.

How can all this information be gathered, organized, and presented in an effective manner? Evaluating accomplishments and coaching to make improvements should focus on three dimensions of performance: outputs, competencies, and style.

In a discussion of **outputs,** the goal is to review what the person has achieved. Achievements can be documented by answering questions such as:

- What results have been produced by the person assigned the ongoing responsibilities of the job?
- Have specific performance goals been met?
- In achieving performance goals, to what degree have the requirements for effective performance been met?

Documenting outputs is relatively simple if performance goals and requirements have been discussed and negotiated in advance. When that's the case, the discussion can focus on determining whether what actually happened corresponds to what was agreed on previously.

The purpose of discussing **competencies** is to pinpoint the types and levels of expertise required in a given job and to compare the individual's current knowledge and skill levels with those requirements. Competencies can be assessed by answering questions like these:

- What types and levels of thinking skills, business knowledge, interpersonal skills, technical knowledge, and physical skills are required by the job?
- What's the person's actual expertise in each area?
- In which areas are there major gaps between required and actual levels of expertise?
- In what areas or situations have the person's strengths been valuable?
- In what areas or situations have the person's weaknesses caused problems?

Answering these questions will provide detail and focus to a discussion of individual skills and knowledge. Doing so will also help identify what the person did to create success and set the stage for performance improvement and development.

In a discussion of **style,** the goal is to review *how* the person gets things done and what *effect* his or her work behaviors have on others. Whether the person giving feedback likes or dislikes the other person's style should be irrelevant. In order to be objective, the feedback needs to focus on how the person's style affects short- and long-term results and work relationships. These questions will help accomplish that goal:

- What specific behaviors does the person use to get things done that have positive effects on results and key work relationships? negative effects?
- What specific incidents give examples of these behaviors?
- In describing the effects of the behaviors identified, what does it feel like to experience this person's style?
- How might counterproductive behaviors be modified?

Discussing style is no small responsibility. If style is affecting an individual's current job performance or future opportunities, then it's a matter of management ethics to let that person know exactly where he or she stands.

Following these guidelines will help keep you on track, whether you're giving or receiving feedback:

- Initiate formal discussions of performance on a regular basis. If you haven't had such a discussion, ask your manager, team members, and customers to give you formal feedback on your performance outputs, competencies, and style.

- When discussing outputs, consider the results achieved in areas in which you had goals or ongoing responsibilities. If past expectations weren't stated clearly and mutually understood, make sure they are in setting goals for the future.

- When discussing competencies, be sure that expectations about skills and knowledge relate to the work that must be done. Feedback about skill and knowledge gaps should be specific.

- When discussing style, acknowledge and neutralize personal biases as much as possible. All specific style behaviors that are discussed should have a demonstrable and direct impact on performance quality or key work relationships.

Although the thought of giving or receiving performance feedback often provokes short-term anxiety, the long-term payoffs are worthwhile for everyone involved. People who give feedback will organize their thoughts in ways that facilitate planning and decision making. And people who receive feedback will know exactly how their contributions are valued and in what specific directions they should work to improve their performance.

▲ Where Do You Stand?

Following the guidelines in this chapter can help improve your feedback practices and reduce your fear of feedback discussions. Suggestions and tips alone, however, can't change the fact that feedback communication is hard work. Accept this fact and set your mind to do the following:

- Continuously improve your feedback communication.

- Concentrate on giving *and* receiving feedback. No one's ever perfect at feedback communication, but being good at it brings many rewards, including better performance and relationships.

- Use good feedback practices whenever you can. Many people expend a lot of energy avoiding feedback situations. Use every opportunity to practice and improve your skills with family, friends, and colleagues. Try out new skills and approaches in different situations, on and off the job. In time, you'll see improvement in feedback skills and results, which should make you feel more comfortable and confident.

Think about your own feedback practices, as sender and as receiver. Consider the questions that follow, and evaluate where you stand:

- **As a receiver, to what extent do you:**

  ____ Ask for feedback when you want or need it?

  ____ Ask for more specific information when you get vague feedback (either positive or negative)?

  ____ Allow your emotions (especially self-defensiveness) to get in the way of hearing and responding to information when you get negative feedback?

  ____ Foster an open communication climate by using receptive skills?

  ____ Use communication games to avoid or derail feedback communication?

- **As a sender, to what extent do you:**

  ____ Regularly check for and set aside your personal biases when you prepare feedback (particularly for formal performance discussions)?

  ____ Hesitate to deliver feedback because of concern for how the receiver will respond?

  ____ Leave feedback discussions feeling that important issues weren't aired?

  ____ Foster an open communication climate by using expressive skills?

  ____ Use communication games to avoid or derail feedback communication?

Based on your answers, what do you most want to improve about your roles as receiver and sender of feedback to make communication more On-The-Level?

▲ Key Points

- *Feedback* is information that can be used to reinforce and improve individual or team performance.

- Many of the common mistakes made in giving and receiving feedback are rooted in emotions, including anxiety and defensiveness.

- In recent years, the increased focus on teams and the need to work across functional boundaries has changed the nature of performance feedback. Today, feedback comes from multiple sources: co-workers, team members, and customers as well as managers.

- Effective feedback is characterized by the Guiding Principles of OTL: directness, respect, shared responsibility, and purpose.

- Six OTL guidelines will help develop effective feedback communication:
  - Think of feedback as information.
  - Organize your thoughts before giving feedback.
  - Ask for feedback.
  - Use a listening template when receiving feedback.
  - Keep the human element.
  - Focus on outputs, competencies, and style.

- The *observation–importance–want* template is useful both in giving and receiving feedback.

- Feedback communication is undoubtedly hard work, but the effort expended is worthwhile in terms of the productivity, trust, and improved work relationships that inevitably result.

CHAPTER 6

Delivering and Digesting Tough Messages

*K*aren has been in her job for several years and has worked closely with the same team for most of that time. Everyone has commented on how well this team works together. Karen would be the first to say that she enjoys her work group; however, she's been wrestling with a persistent problem with one of her associates, John. He's been on the team the longest and helped train her when she started. Overall, he's a talented and friendly co-worker. The last thing Karen wants to do is hurt John's feelings, but she's getting fed up with how he doesn't do his fair share.

John arrives to work late and is the first to leave on most days. In staff meetings, when the "higher ups" are present, he commits the team to doing all kinds of tasks and follow-up on problems. Then, after the meetings, he tells Karen and the other team members to do what he'll ultimately take credit for.

Karen doesn't want to go behind John's back. She owes it to him to talk about her growing frustra-

tion with his work performance. Yet she can't find the words. Driving home at night, when she's most upset about the day's events, she imagines what it would be like to speak her mind to John. Sometimes, she pictures him reacting with wild defensiveness, denying her observations. Other times, she hears John reminding her of how much she owes him for helping her be successful. The worst scenario is deeply hurting John's feelings, to the point that he doesn't want to work with her anymore.

With these unappealing possibilities in mind, Karen decides once again to accommodate John, overcome her frustration, and pretend that nothing's wrong.

▲ Common Problems

Variations on Karen's problem happen everyday: People who work across departmental boundaries hesitate to say what they really think for fear of being labeled "obstructionists." An administrative assistant decides not to share a creative idea because she thinks her manager won't want to make a change or may even take her suggestion as personal criticism. An associate who's technically competent but has an abrasive style that negatively affects team performance is never told about the problem because everyone, including his manager, is afraid of his reaction.

Instead of focusing on how to deliver what very well may be a tough message for someone else to hear, many people go home every night with their stomachs tied in knots. And then, they complain to their friends and family about the "people problems" at work. Ironically, in many instances, these people outside work know more about the problems than the people who are considered to be the problems!

It's easy to say that we should take responsibility for discussing and resolving problems as soon as they become apparent. But in practice, it's not that simple. Other issues enter in, complicating the situation and making performance communication difficult:

- The person on the receiving end of the feedback may have a history of defensive or emotional reactions when confronted with problems.
- The trust level between the people involved may be low, which will make any feedback seem risky.
- The person giving the feedback may have difficulty putting his or her message into words or may fear being misunderstood.

When faced with complications such as these, the task of addressing a problem turns into one of delivering a tough message. Lacking the skills to prepare and deliver that message, people commonly make these mistakes:

- *Rationalization*—Both the people sending and receiving feedback often rationalize their roles and responsibilities in the situation. For instance, the sender might try to avoid giving a tough message by claiming that there are mitigating circumstances (perhaps a lack of time or personnel) or out of fear that misunderstanding might result. The receiver, on the other hand, is likely aware of the problem (even without being told) and will have prepared a million reasons as to why he or she isn't the cause. With both parties attempting to avoid responsibility, the problem may never be discussed.

- *Exacerbation*—Usually, when a problem isn't discussed in the early stages, the situation gradually gets worse, and the problem grows into a crisis. Once more, the involved parties may try to rationalize their roles in what happened, regardless of what they knew or did along the way. The parties may also take or place blame. A manager, for instance, might feel that it's his or her fault that a problem wasn't resolved earlier. Perhaps feeling guilty, he or she might think it unfair to deliver a tough message to staff members and thus give feedback that's not sufficiently clear. The staff can use the fact that the problem wasn't discussed before as an issue in itself. What's more, if the feedback they receive has been toned down, they still won't have heard the real message. The blaming that goes on may mean that the real issue will never be discussed.

- *Avoidance*—When someone wants to give feedback but continually avoids doing so, frustration will build to the point of intolerance. Then, the sender may suddenly confront the receiver and try to resolve the issue in one conversation. The element of surprise doesn't enhance problem solving. In fact, the exchange that results may be too emotional to be productive. After feeling frustrated for so long, the sender will be venting, rather than giving constructive feedback, and the receiver will likely be caught off guard by this sudden development. It's also naive to think that a problem that has existed and gone unaddressed for a long time can be quickly resolved; matters will probably be more complicated than that.

- *One-Sided Action*—Often, feedback givers try to legislate improvements in performance without involving receivers in planning the action or getting their commitment to it. Not surprisingly, such efforts are usually futile. If receivers don't personally commit to changing their behavior and its results, even the best of action plans will be useless. Regardless of commitment, if people lack the skills or support to implement the plan, the effort will again be useless.

Most of the problems described here are variations of the communication games described in Chapter 2. When people perceive that they have to give or receive tough feedback, they use games to put up smoke screens and help avoid what they fear will be uncomfortable or painful. In the end, however, avoiding difficult performance communication situations almost always makes them worse.

Discussions of performance problems or issues that might have serious consequences are especially tough to handle. Here are some common examples of situations involving tough messages:

- Unless an individual's performance improves, he or she will lose a customer or receive an unsatisfactory performance rating, involuntary demotion, or notice of termination.

- Because of increased competition, performance standards have been raised, so that an individual's performance that would've been rated satisfactory in the past is no longer sufficient.
- A staff member isn't able to do his or her job because of something a more senior person is doing or not doing, yet upward feedback is at best, discouraged, and at worst, punished.
- An associate performs his or her job skillfully but has a working style that's proven repeatedly to obstruct communication and problem solving.
- Tension and conflict occur when projects cross organizational boundaries, making it difficult for individuals to discuss problems in a way that's not perceived as blaming or defensive.

These situations have a number of factors in common. What makes messages tough to give and receive?

- People are uncomfortable making judgments and evaluations that will have serious consequences for others.
- Senders fear being met with defensive responses and counterattacks.
- Individuals don't feel comfortable or skilled enough to give feedback to people in authority, such as managers or customers.
- The problem that needs to be discussed is difficult to describe or quantify, such as a work-style issue.
- Receivers are caught totally by surprise, and whatever trust existed in the relationship is destroyed.
- Individuals have had bad experiences giving or receiving feedback, and those learned reactions override their communication skills.
- People simply don't see situations in the same way or have dramatically different values that affect how they evaluate what's happened.
- Raising the issue may very well make a bad situation worse.
- There's no clear way of solving the problem or otherwise improving the situation.

Recognizing where the difficulty lies can be an important first step in preparing to deliver or receive a tough message. Even more importantly, you must get past the emotion that's blocked taking action.

Keep in mind that although delivering tough messages may involve some risks, *not* delivering them may also involve risks. Unresolved issues can have an enormously oppressive effect, influencing the morale, productivity, and well-being of a few individuals, a team or department, or an entire company.

▲ Guidelines for Successful Communication

The tougher the message, the more you'll need to consciously integrate the OTL Guiding Principles of directness, respect, shared responsibility, and purpose. The following suggestions will help you keep discussion channels open and direct when delivering and receiving tough messages. These suggestions are consistent with what you've already read about feedback; however, they focus on difficult situations:

1. Don't wait. Discuss problems before they become crises.
2. Define your view of the problem or relationship before discussing it.
3. When receiving a tough message, focus on active listening.
4. Consciously use your Observing Participant.
5. Focus the discussion on the problem, not the person.
6. Get both sides involved in developing action.

1. Don't Wait. Discuss Problems Before They Become Crises

The most common way people deal with performance problems is to avoid them and hope they'll go away. Whenever serious issues are raised, people typically say, "I knew this was a problem a long time ago, but we never really talked about it."

Hindsight always makes it easier to draw such conclusions, but a lesson should be learned from this experience: Don't wait to deal with work relationships that have gotten off track. Resolving any problem at an early stage—before game playing and avoidance have become recurring patterns—will benefit everyone. Prompt and specific action will also prevent the problem from growing to dimensions that will eventually require serious and extreme solutions.

Everyone has a responsibility to initiate discussions about performance. A manager is responsible for recognizing and addressing performance problems immediately. This responsibility doesn't depend on technical or professional stature, nor does it require extraordinary judgment or evaluation skills (although all managers should continually refine their ability to draw conclusions about performance). Rather, the responsibility to address performance problems is a key part of the role of a manager. Failure to confront staff performance issues is itself a performance problem.

Staff members also have responsibilities. They're accountable for their own performance. If performance goals are clear and the indicators of successful performance have been discussed, then staff members have their own "measuring stick" with which to determine the quality of performance. Because staff members are closest to their own performance and managers aren't often present when staff do their jobs, staff may be in the best position to raise performance problems. In addition, staff members are more likely to act on feedback and problem solutions if they initiate the discussion. Self-evaluation should be an appropriate performance responsibility of all staff members.

Raising issues early also benefits relationships in teams and with colleagues across departments and functions. As bad as communication sometimes is between managers and their staff, most work climate surveys indicate that feedback and communication among *peers* is often worse. Communication at this level is least likely to be addressed, it seems.

The reason may be that competitiveness and/or relationships among peers and organizational issues associated with cross-functional relationships raise the stakes in these situations. Nonetheless, any problem that seems bad in the early stages will probably get worse quickly when it's ignored. Communication among peers at work depends on the same On-The-Level skills and guidelines that help manager/staff member communication.

Discussing problems immediately, before they become crises, requires the efforts of everyone who may be involved. Here are some specific recommendations:

- If you find that you're avoiding certain issues, ask what might be getting in the way:
  - Are you concerned about making judgments?
  - Do you fear being attacked or counterattacked?
  - Are you worried about what consequences the solution may have?

  In answering these questions, be honest about yourself and your concerns. Be respectful of feelings, but also put your energy into preparing and delivering a clear, responsible message.

- Don't wait. As soon as you have a substantive message to deliver, set a time to discuss it. When the issue is identified at an early stage, this discussion can be one in which questioning and listening are as prevalent as sharing your observations. Also, at this early stage, emotions are less likely to run high, which will also contribute to having a productive discussion.

- As the receiver, ask for feedback if you sense that something's wrong. Be alert to signs, such as sudden behavioral changes by your co-workers, your manager, or your staff members. They may have something important to talk about and not know how to begin. Rather than let the problem (and the tension) go on, speak up. Ask what's wrong.

- When you realize that a key performance result won't be met, talk about what it'll take to get back on track, and then set up specific actions to achieve those new goals. Even if you just have a hunch that a problem exists, talk about it rather than hope it'll go away. Again, in the early stages, you'll probably have more and easier solutions.

Regardless of who initiates the discussion, the best time to give and receive feedback is when the problem first appears. The first and most important recommendation for dealing with situations that require tough messages is: Don't wait. Talk about problems before they become crises.

2. Define Your View of the Problem or Relationship Before Discussing It

The way we choose to manage a performance problem or influence a work relationship can have a profound impact on the likelihood that the problem will be resolved and can also affect the level of trust in the relationship. Making a demand—such as "Stop trying to derail this project!"—asserts a solution before a problem has been defined and understood. By not providing adequate information and a chance for open discussion, the person giving the tough message may be setting up a volatile and defensive situation.

The stakes in situations like this are usually high enough to warrant planning by both parties in the feedback exchange. For the sender, planning involves clarifying concerns and getting examples of the other person's actions in specific situations. The sender should also acknowledge and review his or her own biases and how they may affect interpretations and conclusions about the other person and the magnitude of the problem.

In Chapter 5, "Giving and Receiving Feedback," one of the suggestions for communicating On-The-Level was to organize your thoughts before giving feedback. We proposed an organizational template, or structure, outlining three parts of the feedback message:

1. What have I *observed* that makes me want to give feedback?
2. Why are the observations I've described *important* (in terms of performance results)?
3. What do I *want* to happen?

In the case of a tough-message situation, it may be useful to take out a piece of paper and actually write out your answers to these questions. After you've finished, set the paper aside; then pick it up a few minutes or even several hours later. Typically, when you come back to your thoughts, you'll find better and often fewer words to capture what you want to say. You'll also have a chance to edit your thoughts, removing any emotional or judgmental language.

Putting your thoughts in writing will also make you be specific and focused about the purpose and direction of your feedback. By preparing in this manner, you'll gain confidence in your message and your ability to deliver it, which should help overcome your anxiety about being able to penetrate the defense mechanisms of the other person. Remember that as the sender, your role is to prepare and deliver the message.

When you're the receiver, your role in exchanging feedback is to listen to and understand the message. (How to listen for understanding is covered in the next section.) Before the exchange, however, you should pay attention to signs that there may be a problem. For instance, if a special meeting has been set, you should be aware that the message to be delivered might be difficult to hear.

As the sender, once you've decided to face a tough feedback situation, resist the "knee-jerk" reaction to dive in and start talking. Take as much time as you can to think about and prepare your message. Use the *observation–importance–wants* template to organize your thoughts and perhaps even your delivery (see Chapter 5). Also follow these tips:

- If you have several pieces of feedback to give, select the most important point and develop it. You're not ready to give feedback unless you can answer the three questions in the *observation–importance–wants* template.

- Consult a third party to review your message if you have strong biases that may affect your objectivity about the person you'll give feedback. This review will test the validity of your observations in a sort of trial run, before you present them to the other person. It'll also give you more time to think about what you want to say.

- Ask yourself what the consequences will be if the problem continues. Will it lead to a performance problem? Will it seriously damage an important work relationship? You may need to discuss concerns explicitly as you describe the importance of your observations, for example, saying, "I am worried that this feedback will get in the way of our positive relationship."

- If you're dealing with a potential long-term problem, document the actual conversation. If you've used the feedback template, you'll have a good organizational tool for writing up a performance issue for your file, if this is necessary. And if the person receiving the feedback gets it in writing, he or she might take it more seriously. At the very least, you'll both be working with the same information.

3. When Receiving a Tough Message, Focus on Active Listening

So far, most of the recommendations for dealing with tough feedback have been directed to the sender. What about the receiver?

When someone says to you "We need to talk" or "Let's set a time to talk about how things are going," you may realize that you're about to receive feedback. Immediately, your defense mechanisms will swing into action. We can't help having defensive reactions; after all, we're human. But as soon as we notice what's happening, we can make some decisions to override our emotions.

One way to focus your attention on a constructive action, rather than a defensive response, is to make **active listening for understanding** the primary purpose of your communication. Active listening, described in Chapter 5, can only be effective if the goal is to *understand,* rather than to evaluate or decide whether to agree. This is a very important distinction. Specifically, you're separating what's objective—the information—from what's subjective—your reaction to it. By practicing active listening, you can prevent a difficult situation from escalating.

You can also use the three-part template, described in the previous section, as a tool to help you listen. As the sender begins to give you feedback, you may find it hard to follow what he or she's saying. Use the same three elements of the template to form questions that'll help you explore the other person's feedback:

1. What *observations* have you made that'll help me understand what you're most concerned about?
2. Why is this problem so *important* to you? Why should it also be important to me?
3. What do you *want* to happen differently? What can I do to make those things happen?

If you're having particular difficulty following the sender's message, take the initiative to put the discussion on track by sharing this template with him or her. Working with the same set of questions will help you both. Or use the template to structure the feedback you give in response to the sender, again, perhaps sharing the template when you ask probing questions and listen actively to the responses.

Active listening for understanding is an excellent approach to blocking defensive reactions from taking over when you're about to receive feedback. To fine-tune your active-listening skills:

- Try to be aware of your defense mechanisms engaging when you expect to receive feedback. Even if you can't control your reactions at first, focus on the need simply to *understand* what the other person is saying. Try to let go of the need to evaluate, determine right or wrong, or offer counterfeedback. Just listen.

- Use the feedback template and proposed questions to guide the discussion and help you stay in an active-listening mode.

- Resist the temptation to respond immediately to the sender in order to "even the score." If you have feedback to give, take the time to plan your message and ensure that it's a substantive one, not an attempt at revenge.

4. Consciously Use Your Observing Participant

Chapter 3 described the role of the **Observing Participant** during conversation. You may recall that conscious use of the Observing Participant gives you the ability to stay aware of what's happening during a conversation in order first, to think about the purpose of the interaction and then, to choose the communication skills that will keep the discussion on track.

Whether you're the sender or the receiver, there's no better time to use the Observing Participant than in a tough feedback situation. The irony is that the Observing Participant is most difficult to access in these very situations, when we need it most. The reason for this difficulty is that fear, anxiety, and discomfort about a problem situation or relationship take up so much of our energy that we don't have enough in reserve to engage our Observing Participant. Once more, emotions get in the way of effective performance communication.

In reality, though, each of us has the capability of developing the Observing Participant. The first few times you try to engage this role, you may not believe you can do it. But eventually, you'll be able to better focus your mental energy to stay on purpose. Once you achieve that focus, you'll be able to consciously select the communication skills that will most help you in a particular conversation.

5. Focus the Discussion on the Problem, Not the Person

Tough-message situations often come about because the issue that needs to be discussed is difficult to describe in concrete terms. Style issues almost always fall into this category. For instance, there may be a consensus among team members that one team member has a cold manner that affects relationships with others, including customers. But a request to describe what constitutes being "cold" would likely produce as many different answers as team members. Perhaps some of these responses would be specific and founded on actual observations, but others would likely be personal and even judgmental in nature. Overall, it would be difficult to produce a comprehensive, objective view of the problem.

When the issue is one of performance, it's simply not constructive or appropriate to make broad, unsubstantiated, negative statements about an individual and then hope that he or she will improve. Likewise, in situations involving peer relationships or upward feedback, performance communication ceases to be On-The-Level when the message loses purpose, directness, and respect.

Remarks such as the following aren't appropriate in any situation:

- "You're impossible to get along with."
- "No one wants to listen to someone who's patronizing and arrogant, even if they're right."
- "You're not a team player."
- "Our customers expect us to act like professionals, and that's not how I would describe your behavior."

When feedback presents generalizations, judgments, and labels, it becomes a personal attack. Instead of focusing on the problem, the feedback focuses on the person. How does this happen?

We tend to take specific observations and quickly distill them in our minds in order to simplify our thinking process. Then we forget the specific examples our thinking is based on and remember only the conclusions we've drawn. So when we reach into our thoughts for something to say, we end up blurting out a generalization, judgment, or label.

When this happens, the receiver hears only our conclusion—not any of the data the conclusion is based on. If, on the other hand, the sender supplies specific observations of behavior and explains the importance or effect of that behavior, the feedback focuses on the problem again, not the person.

Consider the example of Lynette, whose personal style was considered "cold" by team members and customers. In delivering feedback to Lynette, Byron, the team leader, should describe what he means by "cold" and then provide several specific examples of that behavior. Byron could say:

Lynette, I'd like to pass on some observations about your personal style in communicating with people that may help you be more effective. Your manner sometimes seems cold—in other words, abrupt or unfriendly. Let me give you some examples of what I mean.

In our last meeting, when I gave you several suggestions about the project, you shrugged your shoulders and said nothing in response. I was unsure of how you felt about my suggestions and how you were going to proceed with the project. Some response from you—even something like "I'll have to get back to you on that"—would've been helpful.

I also heard from Carla, one of our customers, who said you ended a phone conversation abruptly, saying that you were too busy to talk to her. Carla needed a quick answer to a question, and when you put her off, it meant she couldn't finish her report. I understand that it's difficult to get things done when the phone keeps ringing, but it's impor-tant that our custom-ers know we're here to help them. If you're really too busy to take a phone call, use your voice mail to re-direct the call to an-other team member or to take a message.

Any feedback discussion in which the purpose is to change behavior is really trying to influence *future* behavior. Feedback of this type isn't given to seek revenge, to punish, or to instill guilt or shame. It's intended to solve a problem. Keeping this objective purpose in mind should help keep the feedback discussion focused on problem solving. The following strategies will reinforce this purpose:

- When you plan and write out your feedback using the template, make sure that your observations are specific examples of behavior, not generalizations, judgments, or labels.

- When giving feedback, if you find yourself saying "You are . . ." (or even if this is implied), stop and think for a minute about how the other person will hear what you're going to say. Most likely, he or she will take your feedback as a generalization or judgment. Think about what your conclusion is based on, and then give that example.

- Focus on your ultimate goal for change: What do you want to accomplish as a result of this communication? This will take your mind off irrelevant needs for evening the score, venting, or punishing the other person.

- Even in addressing style issues, you should be able to identify behaviors and effects that illustrate the problem. The goal is to talk about the problem, not the person.

It's not always easy to be objective and fair, particularly in emotional and high-stakes situations. As human beings, we all have personal needs and agendas, which means we're all prone to making issues personal at times. The key isn't to deny this but to recognize and work on both the personal and the substantive issues.

6. Get Both Sides Involved in Developing Action

One of the problems described in the beginning of this chapter was trying to legislate improvements in performance without involving the person or people affected. Sometimes, a problem produces a lot of frustration and impatience for action, especially if a small problem has become a big one and the people involved have been waiting for resolution. The person giving the feedback may try to resolve the problem in one conversation and demand that the receiver take immediate action. The receiver, however, may not see the situation in the same way. In fact, he or she may have important information beyond the feedback that would change the feedback giver's view.

Even if the receiver doesn't have new information, he or she may simply have a different value or sense of urgency about the problem.

Let's consider Lynette again. In response to the feedback from one of their customers, suppose Byron, the team leader, just hands down a set of guidelines for telephone procedures, without discussing Lynette's personal style. He assumes that by telling her how and when to talk on the phone, her performance will improve. The fact is, Lynette may not be cold but simply shy and lacking self-confidence. If so, she'll likely find Byron's directive intimidating and even hurtful, particularly when it's delivered without explanation or opportunity for discussion. As a result, Lynette may become even more withdrawn and timid—or more cold, in others' eyes. In short, the action Byron took to improve Lynette's performance may make it worse.

Forcing the receiver to accept the opinion that action needs to occur won't lead to meaningful follow-up. Before any commitment to action can occur, agreement must be reached on what happened and why it matters.

The only way to engage the receiver in problem solving and to involve him or her in taking action is to use receptive as well as expressive communication skills. For example, in an attempt to improve Lynette's performance, Byron could use describing to relate what he and others have observed and questioning to draw out information about her views. If he were successful in getting Lynette to open up, he could then use receptive skills, listening to her view of the situation and showing empathy for her concerns. Once all this information is out in the open, Byron and Lynette can work together on a plan to improve her performance.

Using both types of communication skills is a challenge in situations in which avoidance has led to high levels of anxiety about the problem. The tendency is to *overuse* expressive skills and *underuse* receptive skills. This is especially true in situations in which a manager or customer has to address a performance problem. In approaching Lynette, if Byron anticipates that she'll be defensive, he might talk too much, in effect, shutting her out. By doing so, he'll attempt to *control* rather than *participate in* the discussion.

Although it's the manager's responsibility to express a clear view of the problem and the consequences of not resolving it, it's the staff member's job to plan and implement actions for self-improvement and development. Thus, the staff member's commitment to action and ability to act are key to solving the problem. If the staff member doesn't personally commit to changing his or her behavior and its results or if he or she can't carry out an action plan due to lack of skills or resources, then improvement plans will be useless.

Staff member commitment can come from any of the following:

- The staff member feels respected and heard and is engaged in dialogue with the other person.
- The staff member wants to do a good job.
- The staff member wants to achieve what he or she's committed to.
- The staff member doesn't want to suffer the certain negative consequences of doing nothing.

At the end of a discussion about performance problems, the manager and staff member should check out the staff member's commitment to take action. If the staff member decides to help shape the plan for action and then follows through, the discussion has been successful. Another possibility is that the staff member may influence the manager's thinking, and together, they might agree on a new view of the problem and potential solutions. This would also constitute a successful discussion. The final possibility would be that the staff member doesn't agree to the plan or commit to any follow-up action. While this might not feel like a successful discussion, at least the manager and staff member will be able to talk about the consequences of this outcome.

In tough-message situations, it's vital to check the other person's point of view several times, verifying his or her "take" on the points that have been discussed. Both senders and receivers need to be aware of their roles and what they can do to reach agreement and joint involvement in developing action:

- Senders need to become aware of overusing expressive skills. The Observing Participant can help them realize that they need to ask questions and listen as well as relate their points of view.

- Receivers should be asked during and at the ends of discussions to summarize what they see as the problems, consequences, and possible action steps.

- Senders should recognize that receivers have the right not to agree. Each party should try to explore and understand the other person's point of view. It's better to address these differences directly than to pretend that agreement and commitment have been obtained.

- Receivers must remember that they have the opportunity to influence discussions about defining and solving problems.

- When a solution can't be reached in a single discussion, the sender and receiver should take the time to think about other ideas. It's important, however, to be specific about when they'll get together again to finish the discussion so that follow-up action can begin.

▲ Where Do You Stand?

Situations that require delivering and digesting tough messages challenge everyone to make the best possible use of their communication skills. All the guidelines for OTL communication and giving and receiving feedback apply (see Chapter 5). In addition, both senders and receivers need to overcome the anxieties that frequently control both parties when the issues are complex and have the potential for serious consequences.

Resolving tough issues isn't a paper-and-pencil process. It requires face-to-face, voice-to-voice, On-The-Level discussions, sensitivity, and tough-mindedness from both parties. Unfortunately, many people avoid and misunderstand problem situations. Relationships and productivity suffer needlessly when this occurs.

Think about your own feedback practices in giving and getting tough messages. Consider the questions that follow, and evaluate where you stand:

- **As a sender, to what extent do you:**

  _____ Rationalize your role and responsibility in the situation, perhaps trying to avoid giving a tough message?

  _____ Delay delivering tough messages so that they gradually become worse, perhaps even crises, or so that you end up venting out of frustration and even anger?

  _____ Consider your own biases and how they may affect your interpretations and conclusions about the nature and extent of the problem?

  _____ Reflect on the trust level that exists between you and the receiver and how that will impact the message you deliver?

  _____ Give specific and relevant examples of the other person's behavior and what effects it has?

  _____ Legislate improvements in performance without involving the receiver in planning the action or without securing his or her commitment to it?

  _____ Find it difficult to make assessments and deliver information that will have serious consequences for others?

  _____ Fear receiving defensive responses and counterattacks?

  _____ Prepare for delivering a tough message by organizing your message and maybe practicing your delivery?

  _____ Engage your Observing Participant so that you're aware of what's happening before, during, and after the conversation?

- **As a receiver, to what extent do you:**

  _____ Focus on active listening for understanding and avoid evaluating or deciding whether you agree with the message presented?

_____ Recognize your own defense mechanisms engaging when you expect to receive feedback?

_____ Acknowledge a history of negative and emotional reactions to receiving feedback?

_____ Understand that the person giving feedback may have difficulty putting his or her message into words or may fear being misunderstood?

_____ Recognize the trust level that exists between you and the sender and how that will impact the message you receive?

_____ Rationalize your role and responsibility in the situation by preparing a lot of reasons as to why you're not the cause?

_____ Avoid raising performance issues, even when you sense that a problem exists?

_____ Respond immediately to the message, perhaps "evening the score," or take time to plan your response and ensure that it's substantive and accurate?

_____ Engage your Observing Participant so that you're aware of what's happening before, during, and after the conversation?

Based on your answers, what do you most want to improve about your roles as receiver and sender of tough messages to make communication more On-The-Level?

▲ Key Points

- Most of the mistakes commonly made in giving and receiving tough messages are variations of communication games, in which people put up smoke screens to avoid what they fear will be painful.

- Ultimately, avoiding difficult communication situations almost always makes them worse.

- The toughest feedback exchanges are those involving performance or issues that might hold serious consequences.

- Tough messages, like all communication, should be characterized by the guiding principles of OTL: directness, respect, shared responsibility, and purpose.

- The following guidelines promote communicating On-The-Level in situations that call for delivering or digesting tough messages:
  - Don't wait. Discuss problems before they become crises.
  - Define your view of the problem or situation before discussing it.
  - When receiving a tough message, focus on active listening.
  - Consciously use your Observing Participant.
  - Focus the discussion on the problem, not the person.
  - Get both sides involved in developing action.

- Both senders and receivers need to overcome the anxieties that often control them in tough-message situations.

- Many people avoid and misunderstand problem situations, which causes relationships and productivity to suffer needlessly.

CHAPTER 7

Discussing Learning and Development

John's the 10-year veteran manager of a computer company that's recently reorganized into self-managing teams. The company's also made a difficult shift to paying for skills, rather than for time spent in the job. The changes have been traumatic for John, who's used to being in charge and planning and controlling other people's work. Although his new role hasn't yet been completely spelled out, one of his primary functions will be to support and coordinate the teams, who are clamoring for his help to develop their skills.

Supporting individual development has never been John's strong suit. He knows a lot about what the business requires but not much about how to translate those needs into people-focused plans. Although the self-managing teams have done some preliminary identification of key skills, more needs to be done. Early on, John will need to work with individuals on personal development plans and actions. He knows that his role isn't to develop people but to support them. Several team members have already scheduled time to discuss their personal situations with him.

*What can he say? What should he do? What does it mean to sup-
port others in development?*

*John doesn't have the answers to these questions, but he knows
that he'll soon find himself in one-on-one discussions about personal
development issues. He wants to get ready for them.*

▲ Common Problems

John's dealing with one of the most important personal and organizational issues of our time: developing the capabilities to excel in a
rapidly changing, competitive environment. He's aware enough to
realize his need for personal development (and his expected role in
helping others, too), but he's not sure of how to go about it.

Many people—managers and staff members, teams, customers
and suppliers—don't take learning and development seriously. They
spend very little time planning for it, managing it, and evaluating it.
And they miss the opportunities for learning that occur in unplanned,
surprise moments. Why does this happen?

- *Fear of Learning*—Sometimes, individuals are afraid to admit
  they need or want to develop and learn. They feel that development is only for people who are incompetent. When managers
  or fellow team members communicate this perspective, development actions will be superficial and rarely deal with important needs, issues, and options. And when individuals bring this
  perspective to their own lives, they'll avoid opportunities to
  grow and change.

- *Focus and Application*—Development plans and actions aren't
  always sufficiently compelling and relevant. People may do a
  good job in the initial stages, observing performance and discussing personal capabilities and deficiencies, but then not follow up with development plans that relate to real needs and
  produce specific results. Unless development planning is a good

problem-solving process, the plans and actions that result will likely be shallow and off target—for both individuals and organizations.

- *Exclusiveness*—Formal development programs are sometimes offered as special benefits or even limited to "topped out" associates, as if only high-level personnel merit such individualized attention. When development and learning programs become exclusive, their real purposes are distorted or even lost.

- *Lost Vision*—In order to become good at a skill or to know a lot about a subject, an individual will likely have to study, practice, make mistakes, take time away from work, and risk criticism or even ridicule. During the course of development, short-term inconveniences such as these may obscure long-term payoffs. Many people give up on deliberate attempts at development because the payoffs lose their allure or get lost in the day-to-day shuffle.

- *Need for Outputs*—For many people, learning and development mean hours spent reading books, attending courses and workshops, and completing assignments and projects. In effect, development becomes an activity trap in which people get caught and never move beyond. But development isn't an *activity;* it's an *output.* Unless learning and development activities result in changed performance or capabilities, they're meaningless.

- *Individuality*—Development plans are often designed as though everyone has the same learning style, rather than tailored to individual needs. Some people learn faster and better by doing, whereas others learn best by reading, attending courses and workshops, or watching others perform. In short, the best development plan for one person may not be the best for another.

- *Availability of Resources*—Many people plan in the dark. They set development goals without first taking the time to identify and use the best learning resources available. As a result, the development process is often longer and less focused than it should be, which might lead to some of the other problems mentioned here.

- *Receptiveness*—Finally, many people don't recognize and appreciate the ongoing, widespread nature of learning and development. Opportunities to learn and develop can be found everywhere, all the time. We can develop through acting and observing what happens, making mistakes at times and enjoying successes at others. We can even develop by watching others act and noticing how they handle mistakes and successes. But none of this learning by doing and observing will occur unless we're willing to explore, reflect, and think about cause and effect.

Learning and development are processes of improving your (and ultimately, your organization's) competence and ability to perform. None of us can afford to ignore these processes. Our individual capabilities and the values that drive them must keep up with or stay ahead of change, whether professional or personal. And the fact is, change is inevitable in today's dynamic environment.

▲ Guidelines for Successful Communication

From this perspective, the process of learning and development teaches survival skills as well as enhances personal fulfillment. Given its importance, to individuals and to organizations, this process should be focused on getting the following results:

- Individuals learn continuously—from mistakes and successes, from themselves and others, from formal study and reading as well as everyday events and issues.
- Individuals resolve the performance, skill, style, attitude, and value problems that may be limiting their current and future options.

- Individuals are able to deal with new equipment, technology, systems, structures, processes, and other changes affecting them.
- Individuals have the ability to think creatively and contribute ideas for continuous improvement and innovation.
- Individuals can competently manage life changes that may be affecting job satisfaction and productivity.
- Individuals increase their ability to manage themselves and to work in the environment of shared responsibility/shared power that now characterizes many organizations.

Achieving these results requires the free exchange of information and ideas among people who are open to learning, from whatever the source. Once you've formed this mindset, you need to employ On-The-Level (OTL) principles and skills to manage the communication intrinsic to successful development. Working to improve your OTL communication abilities will also likely increase your respect for and commitment to development as a critical aid to personal satisfaction and productivity.

You can help make sure that performance development discussions produce quality results by following these four guidelines:

1. Tailor actions for the learner.
2. Create a vision.
3. Blend planning and opportunism.
4. Support a learning ethic in all actions.

The first three guidelines focus on achieving planned results through learning and development activities, and the last supports continual scanning and learning from insight and surprise.

1. Tailor Actions for the Learner

For many of us, development is either a random process or one in which we submit to the control of teachers, books, and programs. This is understandable. Learning is a regular part of life, so it's easy to be random and even unconscious of just how much is going on. Also, most of our educational experiences have trained us to follow directions in completing assignments and taking tests; to read books from front to back, because that's how the authors have organized them; and to complete projects and courses according to set plans or programs.

It's understandable, then, why many of us feel stuck, unable to initiate learning and development on our own. That's the problem in this scenario:

Elise works in a fairly traditional retailing organization in which most people feel trapped because of downsizing and increasingly restricted career opportunities. She's been in the same job for three years and wants to explore new opportunities—preferably in the same company. Even expanding her current job would be a welcome change.

Elise has told her manager, Caroline, that she wants to learn more. Caroline's been supportive, but she always speaks in such general terms that she isn't helpful. Elise has also taken lots of courses and read a number of books, but they haven't really provided any answers either.

At this point, Elise doesn't think she can figure things out for herself. She really doesn't know what she wants or where she should start.

Like Elise, many of us equate **deliberate learning** with "going to school," which means that someone else is in charge. This is actually a very old-fashioned view of education. Most educators today acknowledge the importance of identifying individual needs and tailoring opportunities for learning accordingly. For adults, in particular, learning must be deliberate and customized to be successful. The most productive discussions about personal learning and development recognize this.

Much of our learning comes from working with other people. In fact, about one-third of all that we learn is facilitated, in some way, by people who are *not* trained as teachers or counselors. Unfortunately, much of this learning isn't as effective as it could be because **learners** don't know how to use others' support and **helpers** often don't know how to help. Knowing and applying this information about learning can help bring focus and power to OTL development discussions.

In order to sufficiently tailor development plans and actions, both learners and helpers (or people who are learning together) need to understand how the learning process works and what factors affect it.

Learning Is a Process

As a process, learning involves many common steps:

1. Decide what direction to move in (even in general terms).
2. Develop a vision of the end result.
3. Identify what capabilities are or will be important to achieving that vision, including which ones you have and need to develop.
4. Plan actions for development.
5. Find and select the resources needed to carry out the planned actions.
6. Take the planned actions using the selected resources.
7. Assess and acknowledge progress.
8. Deal with barriers, disappointments, mistakes, and inefficiencies.
9. Recognize when to move on to other goals.
10. Celebrate accomplishment.

Development discussions may occur at any of these stages. As a learner, for example, you might ask for help in identifying career directions that fit your values, needs, and skills (step 1); in developing your vision (step 2); or in discussing the capabilities required for success (step 3). You might ask for help in planning actions (step 4) and identifying resources (step 5) or get coaching support while you try things out (step 6). You might ask others to give you feedback on progress (step 7) or want to talk over disappointments, frustrations, and periods of low energy and commitment (step 8). Or you might use conversations with others to help you formally close a learning project (step 9) or to consciously celebrate success (step 10).

The key point in this scenario is that the learner must be in charge of the entire process. In OTL development discussions, the learner is a responsible participant, with few exceptions. Even in training situations, in which a teacher or facilitator takes charge of most of the steps in learning, the learner is still responsible for making sure that his or her needs and abilities are addressed. As much as possible, the learner should guide the pace of instruction, opportunities for discussion versus practice, and exchange of feedback. For example, a pilot in training will be under the careful direction of an instructor. But the trainee must ensure that he or she gets the information needed, presented in the right way, in order to learn.

The helper's role is to be a sounding board and to bring to the learner whatever knowledge he or she has about the organization, the situation, the learner, and learning itself. If the helper doesn't have specific information relevant to a certain step in the learning process, he or she can help by pointing out that now's the right time to take that step. When the time comes to think about what resources are available, for example, the helper might point out the need to do so but defer to someone else, even the learner. In that case, the helper's role isn't that of "content expert" but "sounding board" and "observer."

The latter are highly important roles, to be sure. A helper who's sympathetic and honest and who uses good receptive communication skills is as valuable (and sometimes more helpful) as one who knows everything about a topic but doesn't empathize, listen, or observe. Most of us have had teachers who clearly knew their subject but weren't very effective in helping others learn it. Like all effective performance communication, learning is an *exchange* of information, not a *transmission*. Learning requires both receptive and expressive skills.

Research indicates that the learning process is most likely to break down in steps 2, 3, 5, 8, and 9. So these are the times when development discussions can have really great impact. Getting help and support from others at these times can bring fresh energy and commitment to your plan or project, perhaps even saving it. At the very least, an OTL discussion can give you a reality check on the status of development—what's been done, what needs to be done, and so on.

Clearly, knowing the steps involved in learning can bring rigor and focus to development discussions. Working with steps breaks down what's otherwise an often abstract and unwieldy process, thus making the process understandable and manageable. Before an OTL development discussion even starts, both parties should agree at what step they are. A productive conversation can proceed from that point.

Learners Have Different Learning Styles

Much has been written about learning styles, and many models have documented how differently people think, what resources they prefer to use, and how introverted and extroverted they are. In the specific context of development discussions, keep several key points in mind:

1. Different individuals are comfortable with different learning styles:
   - Some of us are more **extroverted;** others, more **introverted.** Some prefer action—that is, learning by doing and working with others. Others need to think before they act, to reflect.
   - We vary in our desire to read, to listen, and to observe; to use computers and video- and audiotapes; to learn in a classroom or in real settings; and so on. Our individual differences may be due to past experiences, skill levels, or personality factors. But whatever their origins, they're real.
   - Some of us prefer to synthesize, create, and imagine (that is, to think and learn **inductively**), whereas others would rather analyze, organize, and interpret (to think and learn **deductively**). Inductive processes are often viewed as being random and undisciplined, and deductive processes, as logical and controlled.
   - Some of us easily take charge of our own learning process; others like to rely on others for structure and motivation.

2. A successful development discussion starts by acknowledging that helpers and learners likely prefer different approaches to learning. When that's understood, neither party will impose his or her approach on the other.

3. Both helpers and learners may tend to avoid actions and resources that are unfamiliar or uncomfortable. Sometimes, it's useful to give in to these tendencies, but at other times, greater learning results from taking risks.

In OTL development discussions, we must assume and accept individual differences. Success depends on all of us—learners and helpers—recognizing our own preferences and tendencies and using them in the best way to learn. Specifically, as helpers we must:

1. Be aware of our own style
2. Refuse to impose it on the learner
3. Encourage the learner to stretch, trying new approaches—for example:
   • To use an extroverted rather than an introverted approach
   • To read rather than take a course
   • To try something creative rather than just look over someone else's ideas
   • To ask for support versus trying to control every action

As learners, our self-analysis may mean:

1. Appreciating helpers' style differences
2. Learning from and in spite of them—in this case, empathy and listening tasks become difficult but potentially very stimulating

Learning Outcomes Vary

We engage in the learning process to innovate and create. Ultimately, all worthwhile learning makes us more effective and contributing members of our world, be it the workplace or elsewhere.

On a personal level, learning involves change in one or more areas: knowledge, skills, values and attitudes, and style. When you're trying to be deliberate in learning or helping, it's useful to identify the main area or areas in which you're attempting change:

- If the main area is **knowledge,** then you'll get greatest leverage from finding good information sources, using effective concentration and memory techniques, and learning ways to quickly apply what you've learned.

- If your need is primarily **skill** development, then taking time to practice, get feedback, and sustain yourself through the difficulties of habit change will be key.

- If change is needed in **attitude** or **values,** then it'll be important for you to learn about the negative consequences of old values and attitudes and the positive consequences of new ones, to get facts relevant to a new way of thinking, and to get close to people who have different values and attitudes.

- If you want to change or support a change in **style,** then feedback and making specific and defined behavior changes will be vital.

- To ensure expanded **creativity**, brainstorming, looking for ideas in disciplines outside your own, and using imagination should be your focus.

This list shows that learning and development can occur in many areas. Discussion can help clarify where the main emphasis should be. Either the learner or the helper can address that topic by asking: Is this a knowledge, skill, attitude/value, style, or creativity issue? Once that's been determined, OTL dialogue can proceed.

Learning Is Often Messy

The processes of learning and development, no matter how well organized and supported, are necessarily messy and even disturbing, at times. Part of the difficulty is that change of any sort involves a number of irrational components and raises personal issues—ranging from enjoyment, fulfillment, confidence, and surprise to frustration, defensiveness, confusion, and anger. Experiencing this gamut of emotions is usually necessary for us to achieve true personal change and growth.

Another complication is that learning and development involve not only acquiring new knowledge, skills, attitudes, and behaviors but giving up old ones, as well. For instance, acquiring new knowledge means challenging our old assumptions and values. Developing new skills often demands leaving behind our old and comfortable habits and enduring periods of incompetence while trying out those skills. In sum, any real change has the potential to disrupt our relationships, our goals, our habits, and even our sense of competence. While we're learning, it's not unusual to feel defensive, angry, and disconnected.

In other words, deep learning often plunges us into the "belly of the whale," so to speak. When this happens, support for development is vital. The purpose of support isn't to smooth over our discomfort but to encourage us to accept and use it, to move with and through it. Empathy, listening, and restating the overall learning goals are key OTL actions in this situation. Both learners and helpers must avoid the temptation to retreat or to fix.

For example, a person who has just learned basic skills in a new word-processing program may be frustrated with his or her mistakes and dependence on the manual. Support discussions should encourage the individual to take time to learn the new program, rather than retreat to the old one. Likewise, support discussions should help the individual learn to solve his or her own problems when they occur, rather than depend on others to do so.

It's difficult to discuss development and tailor it to individual needs when the parties involved don't understand what learning and development are. To reiterate:

- Learning is a process.
- Learners have different learning styles.
- Learning outcomes vary.
- Learning is often messy.

2. Create a Vision

Some people believe in **self-fulfilling prophecy:** that if you know what you want to achieve and set out to achieve it, you'll succeed. When they're successful, such personal visions have a few key features in common:

- They solve important problems, meet important needs, and connect with important goals.
- They provide pictures of success in situations that you anticipate will happen or want to be part of.
- They focus on the end state, not on the actions needed to get there.
- They're shared with trusted stakeholders who can provide support (or serve as barriers) along the way.

Consider an example of developing personal vision:

Catherine is a data-processing consultant who has terrific ideas for solutions to user problems. She has a difficult time communicating her ideas, though, because she's shy and easily intimidated. Realizing these limitations, Catherine decided to ask for help from Anthony, a colleague who's more aggressive in his performance communication:

"My shyness is getting in the way of my success and happiness at work. You do well at work communicating with our customers. Will you help me get better at this?"

Fortunately for Catherine, Anthony knows how to help others develop. Initially, he spent several hours with her, helping her "jump into the future" by describing situations in which she wants to be competent, supportive, and influential.

He asked her to imagine situations in the future, first dealing with less intimidating customers and then with really challenging ones. He guided her through descriptions of the meeting places, the business problems and issues, and her reactions and feelings as a successful consultant. He asked her to imagine the challenging questions that would be asked, the competent responses she would provide, and the positive reactions her customers would give. He helped her think about and feel what it would be like after having a successful meeting.

Now that Anthony is sure Catherine has a vision of success, they'll begin to identify the skills she needs and the actions she'll take to move forward.

Under today's fast-paced conditions, action plans often change. Your plan to take a course, complete a developmental assignment, read a book, or try a new technique can quickly be derailed. But if you have a vision of personal development, you can always find another path and create new opportunities. Of course, your vision can and often will change, but it will be far more stable than any of the actions involved in accomplishing it.

Discussion can play an important role in establishing a vision. Just talking about your vision with someone else often stimulates new ideas. Others might have insights, observations, and questions that will make your vision richer and more real. OTL development discussions that focus on visions harness powerful forces for change. It's often true that our perceptions and expectations shape and create the world, rather than the opposite.

3. Blend Planning and Opportunism

In the past, concerns for development have usually emphasized **development plans.** When these plans have been created, however, they've often fallen apart, due to conflicting priorities, lack of commitment, or necessary changes in need or situation. Because of these experiences, many of us feel that development planning sounds like a good idea but doesn't work in the real world.

Having a vision will bring stability and focus to development planning without imposing impractical constraints. Combining planning with opportunism is another useful way of fostering development—in fact, perhaps the best way available today.

Before considering this blend of planning and opportunism, let's examine each element separately.

Development Plans

Today's best plans answer these questions:

- What's my vision?
- What knowledge, skills, attitudes/values, style, and creative capacity are needed to achieve my vision?
- What knowledge, skills, attitudes/values, style, and creative capacity do I deliberately need to develop?
- What resources will I use, and what actions will I take? approximately when?
- Who will help me? How?
- How will I keep up my energy through the difficult and challenging stages of personal development?
- When do I expect to have achieved my vision? How will I know that I've made it?
- How committed am I to achieving this vision? That is, how important is it to me? Why?

A development plan becomes real only when you've truly committed to it. So if your answer to the last question about degree of commitment is "not very," you should find another idea and work on a new vision. Life is too short to spend pursuing ideas and visions that aren't important to you.

Writing out your commitment on paper may help you feel its significance, too. But keep in mind that the paper isn't the plan nor does making this gesture mean that you'll accomplish the plan. Holding development discussions can also help you declare and test your commitment as well as help refine your plan. OTL skills and principles will again provide tools for successful performance communication.

Opportunism

Learning and *change* go hand in hand. They stimulate each other, creating a cycle of personal growth. The effective learner knows this and uses change to his or her advantage.

Every day, new situations and opportunities arise: projects occur, problems surface, customers' needs change, books and workshops are presented, magazines come across the desk, new people are met, capabilities are realized, and even songs inspire insights. The best learners are always alert to resources and opportunities that can help move them toward their vision—or even create new visions. Likewise, the best helpers find new resources to recommend, additional support ideas to share, and so on.

For both learners and helpers, the key to *responding* to opportunity is *recognizing* it. Visions and plans—and the discussions that shape and test them—prepare people to recognize opportunities as they arise. Think about Arthur's case:

Arthur's a staff accountant for a public relations firm who really wants to move into the advertising side of the business. He's spent a lot of time thinking about the difficulty of making that shift and has created a pretty good vision of the kind of work he wants to do. He's also spent some time talking to his wife about the knowledge, skills, attitude, and style of learning he already has and what he'll need to work on to achieve his vision. He's started work on an action plan and feels on track.

A few days before going on vacation, Arthur spoke briefly to Linda, a mentor at work, about his vision and action plan, sharing some ideas he has for making the transition. Linda supported the change and agreed to keep Arthur in mind in her own planning.

While on vacation, as he began to settle into island life, Arthur found that his "antenna" were picking up many signals he probably would've ignored in the past. He found himself critiquing billboards and studying ads in travel magazines. On his way out of the hotel, he noticed a small announcement of a local half-day seminar by a prominent expert in mass psychology. When he drifted into a bookstore to buy a detective novel, he noticed one book about an accountant- turned-mystery- writer and another on advertising in the information age. When he called in to check his voice - mail, there was a mes- sage from Linda, who had good news about a small project he could work on to develop some experience in new areas.

All of a sudden, Arthur's world seemed flooded with resources and support for his new vision.

Arthur's experience isn't unique. Many of us are surprised to find that resources to support development are everywhere. They're sometimes disguised or invisible to unaware eyes, but they're always there. Having development discussions can help raise our awareness of resources as we consider our needs and those of others and commit to acting when opportunities occur.

4. Support a Learning Ethic in All Actions

Support for continuous learning and improvement and creation of a learning organization are common goals in today's workplace. But what do these goals mean on a practical level? And what role does OTL communication play in achieving them?

Jackson is working in a rapidly growing telecommunications com- pany, which is trying to be on the cutting edge in combining voice,

imaging, and data technologies. His company stresses being a learning organization, in which people learn from mistakes as well as successes, in which they constantly benchmark "best practices" in other companies, and in which departments are encouraged to educate each other.

People in Jackson's company are rewarded for helping make it a learning organization. But he isn't sure what that means or what he should be doing, either to learn himself or to help others learn.

In part, we create a **learning ethic** by taking deliberate actions to learn and develop in specific areas. The three guidelines for OTL communication discussed earlier in this chapter focus on ways of supporting this type of purposeful learning.

But creating a learning ethic goes beyond taking deliberate actions. It also involves our mindset, our general outlook on life and what it has to offer. Every day, we take actions that have consequences that lead us to new insights. Sometimes, we learn from our successes; other times, from our failures. We also have daily opportunities to learn from others' experiences—their successes and failures.

Life's lessons are sometimes obvious, so that it's pretty easy to figure out what happened and why. But at other times, actions may have strange and unintended effects. This makes determining cause and effect more difficult. When we are perceptive to these odd effects and what likely caused them, we have a big advantage in the learning and development game. Like detectives, we see things that others miss.

Detective-style learning requires taking many courageous actions. We must learn to recognize when things aren't going as expected. We have to be willing to look at things in new ways. We need to give up pet theories and plans that aren't working. We may have to admit for a time that we don't know what's going on. We have to be able to admit to errors and mistakes and be prepared to start over.

Courageous actions like these are difficult to take in an environment in which people are expected to "do it right the first time" or are rewarded for achieving perfection. In a risk-averse culture, there's no room for discovery or experimentation, let alone individuality. Thus, there's no room for learning.

The opposite environment—a **learning organization**—is one in which people talk openly about successes and mistakes, planned and unplanned results. For learners, this development discussion means observing, describing, and concluding about results and their causes. It means questioning assumptions, models, concepts, and plans. It means being willing to admit that some things didn't work as planned and that others had surprising results. It also means finding and studying the best practices and lessons of others and moving beyond the tendency to reject solutions from other sources.

For helpers, the development discussion means encouraging people to talk about successes and failures and to share lessons with others quickly so that problems don't recur. Helpers should ask questions, empathize with feelings of failure and confusion, and listen analytically for lessons that can be repeated. Helpers should add their conclusions to other people's attempts to draw lessons from experience. Helpers can also encourage people to seek and learn from others' experiences.

Conversations about "what we are learning" should be held regularly as a normal part of project and personal performance discussions. Insights from mistakes, dead ends, and surprises should be appreciated and revered, rather than minimized, hidden, and subtly punished. Open dialogue about development fosters rapid learning for individuals and organizations. Although no one can measure the exact economic value of such learning, when it exists as a norm across an organization, it undoubtedly provides a great competitive edge.

▲ Where Do You Stand?

Development is a critical issue for individuals and their organizations. It affects both current success and the potential for success in the future. On-The-Level discussions can significantly improve the quality of development by expanding the range of information and support available to the individuals involved. Both sides of the learning equation—learners and helpers—must play active roles in purposeful, deliberate development.

Think about your own learning and development practices, as learner and helper. Consider the questions that follow, and evaluate where you stand:

- **As a learner, to what extent do you:**

    _____ Understand the steps in the learning process and ask others for ideas and support relevant to your current status?

    _____ Know your own learning style and use your strengths to help you learn?

    _____ Stretch beyond your comfort zone to use alternative resources, approaches, and supports?

    _____ Recognize and respect the different approaches and recommendations of others?

    _____ Turn to others for support during the difficult stages of learning, at least remaining open to others' feedback?

    _____ Find yourself willing to work with others to create, refine, and test your development vision?

    _____ Take charge of your own development process, while using others whenever their support can add value?

    _____ Use an appropriate balance of receptive and expressive skills in conversations about development?

    _____ Watch for and learn from mistakes and surprises as well as successes and planned results?

    _____ Willingly question your own assumptions, change your theories and plans, and admit your mistakes and successes so that others can benefit from your learning?

_____ Incorporate the lessons of others into your actions, learning from their best practices and mistakes as though they were your own?

- **As a helper, to what extent do you:**

_____ Consider what learning is, what steps it requires, and what individual differences will affect progress?

_____ Operate as a sounding board, helping others take and own their own development?

_____ Understand your own learning style and prevent it from unduly biasing your recommendations and support?

_____ Appreciate that learning is often messy?

_____ Help others sustain their energy and hope through the difficult times of learning and change?

_____ Help others clarify and then sustain their visions and plans for success?

_____ Look for resources and opportunities that are relevant to others' learning goals?

_____ Help others learn from their own and other people's experiences, appreciating the learning value offered by failures as well as successes?

Based on your answers, what do you most want to improve about your roles as learner and helper in development discussions to make performance communication more On-The-Level?

▲ **Key Points**

- Many people don't take learning and development seriously. They spend little time planning for it, managing it, and evaluating it and are completely oblivious to seizing unplanned opportunities for learning.

- Individual capabilities and the values that drive them must keep up with or stay ahead of change, which is inevitable in today's dynamic environment.

- You can help make sure that development discussions produce quality results by following these four guidelines:
  - Tailor actions for the learner.
  - Create a vision.
  - Blend planning and opportunism.
  - Support a learning ethic in all actions.

- Development discussions may occur at any stage of the learning process.

- The success of development discussions depends on learners and helpers recognizing their own preferences and tendencies and using them appropriately to get learning results.

- On a personal level, learning involves change in one or more areas: knowledge, skills, values and attitudes, and style.

- The process of learning and development, no matter how well organized and supported, is necessarily messy and even disturbing, at times.

- For both learners and helpers, the key to *responding* to opportunity is *recognizing* it.

- In a risk-averse culture, there's no room for discovery or experimentation, let alone individuality; thus, there's no room for learning.

CONCLUSION

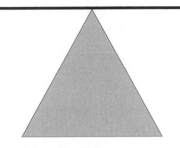

Al hung up the phone for the last time in what had been a tough week. He was ready to go home, work out, and then take off for a relaxing four-day vacation. This week had been one of his most satisfying as a team leader, in spite of several difficult moments.

First, Maria, one of the team's most experienced members, had told the team she might want to extend a deadline because the sales department hadn't provided the information she needed to make a key advertising decision. Fortunately, Al's past encouragement to employees to "stop problems early" had paid off in this case. Maria had taken the task as far as she could and involved Al when she ran into a problem she thought he could help handle. Al's involvement had been brief and appropriate. Through some tough negotiations with the director of sales, he'd gotten relevant members of the sales group to provide the support needed. The task had been placed back in Maria's hands, and the deadline had been saved.

Then there was the situation with John. In recent months, the team had passed over him for assignments to several important projects.

On Tuesday, John confronted Al with this fact, asking, "Why has the team kept me in the background, Al?"

Even though his anxieties about discussing style issues had been intense, Al felt good about his response:

"John, I guess I've been partly responsible. I'm not comfortable with your abrasiveness in sensitive situations. I think your style has been a key factor in losing two small but potentially important accounts. I haven't seen you spend enough time listening to our customers, understanding what's on their minds."

The ensuing conversation had unearthed a number of issues— ones that had clearly influenced Al's and the team's decisions not to give certain tasks to John. During the discussion, Al confronted John about playing the Wounded Animal, trying to make people feel guilty about their messages to him. Al also admitted to his own tendency to play Detective, asking leading questions to get information.

Clearly, it would've been better if Al had initiated the feedback discussion about John's style as soon as he felt it affecting his decision making. But all things considered, Al felt good about what had happened: John had felt safe raising the issue; both Al and John had admitted to the games that usually interfered with their communication; and Al had been able to express himself and give specific examples during a discussion of the formerly taboo area of John's style.

While driving home, Al thought:

"I've come a long way from my early days as an unassertive junior team member. I used to avoid performance discussions and merely checked boxes on performance reviews. The teams I lead are also taking on much more responsibility for the quality of their own performance and for communication about it. They demand to be clear about goals and roles, and they expect to know where they stand with customers, each other, and me. We've 'unleashed a lion' here by working on everyone's communication skills and attitudes. But it's sure easier to go on vacation, now that I know I'm leaving other responsible people behind—people who can and will deal with issues On-The-Level."

There's no guaranteed formula for achieving successful performance communication. Nothing assures that using high-level communication skills and following key principles will result in increased productivity and satisfaction at work. But common sense and experience suggest otherwise.

Take Al, for example. He didn't have an easy week, to be sure, but he came through it feeling good because he was able to handle the issues he faced effectively. His use of OTL communication skills and principles proved invaluable in problem solving, even in some tough-message situations. And because OTL communication is the norm among his team members, Al can go on vacation without worrying.

In most organizations, managers, staff members, teams, suppliers, and customers don't communicate at the levels necessary for excellent performance. They have different views of what individual performance should be, where it fits into the "big picture," how individuals are doing, and what constitutes major growth and development needs. Worse yet, they don't have the communication tools to uncover and address these differences.

This stalemate in communication doesn't have to be the standard, however. As a responsible participant in the performance communication exchange, you can make your own performance communication more OTL.

How can you do this? Seven factors are key:

1. Imagine yourself in performance discussions in which things are going well. See yourself using receptive and expressive skills. Imagine yourself telling the truth, being respectful, taking responsibility, and moving toward a purpose.

2. Prepare for important performance discussions, whether you're initiating or responding to them. Ask yourself:
   - What do I want from this communication?
   - Do I want a specific message to be heard?
   - Do I know how I'm being seen?

Remember that *directness* is irrelevant without *direction*. You'll not likely accomplish much if you don't know your own priorities. Preparation is vital.

3. Become an astute observer of communication. Observe how others use receptive and expressive skills. Notice what they do when games occur. Try to connect *what* they do with the *results* they get. Become a conscious student of others' person-to-person communication. Then apply those observations to your own communication, sharpening your Observing Participant capability. If you forget to observe yourself during a conversation, try afterward to remember what happened. Keen observation, even after the fact, provides valuable lessons. Eventually, you'll find "observing while communicating" to be easier and more automatic. That's the goal, which may take time to develop.

4. Intend to be helpful to others. As you deliver a message, think about how it's being received. Observe the effects your message has on other people. Think about how you can help them hear what you're saying. And remember that it's easier for others to hear your point of view if they know you have heard theirs.

5. From time to time, rate yourself on the four OTL Guiding Principles. How are you doing on:
   - Directness?
   - Respect?
   - Shared responsibility?
   - Purpose?

   What specific behaviors should you begin to use or use more frequently in order to improve?

6. Seize every opportunity to use good communication skills: observing, empathizing, listening, questioning, describing, and concluding. These skills are important in family, religious, and recreational relationships as well as work relationships. Improving skills in one area will likely cause improvement in the others, too.

7. Your goal should be continuous improvement, not perfection. OTL communication is a human process, not a mechanical one. Unless you can eliminate emotions and uncertainty from com-

munication situations, you'll always face snags and surprises. Having complications like this is the price we pay for being people, not robots.

Imagine success. Prepare. Hone your Observing Participant skills. Be helpful. Be principled. Use every opportunity to strengthen your skills. And accept communication as a human process, with all its complications. These are the ingredients for successful communication at all levels: between managers and staff, among team members, between suppliers and customers, and so on.

And when you think you have a good handle on these ingredients, work even harder: On-The-Level communication can always be improved. The results are well worth the effort!

INDEX

A

action plans
  learning and development and, 147, 154, 155
  tough messages and, 122, 126, 124, 134–137
active listening, 31, 53, 124, 129–130. *See also* listening
activities versus outputs, 78–80, 85–86
Ally Building, 45, 46
annual performance discussions, 103. *See also* performance communication; performance discussions
attitudes/values (as area of learning and development), 150–151, 152, 155

B

biases (personal), 5, 16, 28, 31, 39, 116
"big picture" context, 73–77, 165
body language. *See* nonverbal communication
budget. *See* resources

C

Change the Scent, 44
closed questions, 34, 35, 43
codependency (in the workplace), 18
communication
  effective, 4–6
  games. *See* games (communication)
  intentional vs. random, 6
  interactive nature of, 4, 6, 20, 53
  media-based, 20
  performance. *See* performance communication
  principles of. *See* Guiding Principles (of OTL)
  procedures for, 6, 7
  responsibilities for. *See* customers; managers; organizations; staff members; suppliers; teams
  skills. *See* Communication Skills (of OTL)
  written. *See* written communication
Communication Skills (of OTL), 8, 25–50
  application of, 39–40, 52, 59–60, 166
  balance among, 27–28, 31–32, 33, 39–40, 135
  communication games and, 41, 43, 45–46
  concluding, 27, 33, 38–39, 41, 43, 46, 52, 60, 77, 82, 83, 103, 159, 166
  customer needs and, 77, 84
  describing, 27, 33, 36–38, 39, 41, 43, 46, 52, 53, 60, 77, 83, 103, 135, 159, 166
  empathizing, 27, 28, 32–33, 39, 40, 45, 46, 52, 60, 82, 83, 111, 135, 159, 166
  exchange among, 31–32, 35
  expressive, 27–28, 31–32, 33–40, 43, 60, 77, 83, 84, 100, 135, 137, 148, 165

169

Communication Skills *continued*
feedback and, 100, 101, 103
goal agreement and, 82–84
Guiding Principles and, 26, 27
learning and development and,
145, 148, 155, 159
listening, 27, 28, 30–32, 39–40, 45,
46, 52, 53, 60, 77, 82, 126, 135,
137, 148, 150, 152, 166
observing, 27, 28–30, 31, 45, 46, 52,
60, 77, 148, 159, 166
Observing Participant and, 55,
59–60, 62
outcomes, 39–40
problem solving and, 165
purpose and, 27
questioning, 27, 33, 34–35, 40, 41,
43, 46, 52, 60, 77, 82, 126, 135,
137, 159, 166
receptive, 27, 28–33, 39–40, 60, 77,
83, 84, 100, 135, 148, 165
respect and, 27
shared responsibility and, 27
tough messages and, 126, 131, 135,
137, 165
transition, 35
competencies (personal), 108, 111,
113–116, 142, 144, 152
concluding, 27, 33, 38–39, 41, 43, 46,
166
feedback and, 103
goal agreement and, 77, 82, 83
learning and development and,
159
Observing Participant and, 52, 60
conversation. *See* "STOP" and "SEE"
Model
costs. *See* resources
Counterattack, 45
creativity (as area of learning and
development), 150–151, 152,
155
crises
goal agreement and, 72–73, 88, 89
tough messages and, 121, 124–127
cross-functional teams, 87, 98. *See
also* functional boundaries;
teams

culture
organizational, 6, 14–15, 46, 83–84,
87, 106, 107, 108, 110
social, 40, 46
"customer focus," 75
customers
Communication Skills and, 77, 84
communication with suppliers, 3,
18, 75–77, 82–86, 98, 99, 165
definition of, 75
educating, 82, 83
external, 75
feedback and, 98, 99, 103, 105
focus on, 75
goal agreement and, 70, 71, 74,
75–88
internal, 75
needs/expectations of, 70, 71, 74,
75–77, 82, 84
outputs and, 77–78
quality requirements and, 81–82,
84
resources and, 84
role agreement and, 86–87
tough messages and, 135
value added for, 71, 82, 84

D

deductive thinking/learning, 149
defensiveness
avoiding, 54
communication games and, 41, 42,
43, 45
feedback and, 97–98, 99, 100, 103,
106, 110
goal agreement and, 72–73
Observing Participant and, 54
tough messages and, 127, 128, 129,
130
deliberate learning, 142, 145–146,
150–151. *See also* learning and
development
describing, 27, 33, 36–38, 39, 41, 43,
46, 166
feedback and, 103
goal agreement and, 77, 83
learning and development and,
159

Observing Participant and, 52, 53, 60

tough messages and, 135

Detective, 43

development plans, 142–143, 147, 154–157. *See also* learning and development

directness, 15–17

   communication games and, 43

   definition of, 15–16

   direction and, 166

   expressive communication skills and, 27

   feedback and, 99

   goal agreement and, 91

   Observing Participant and, 52

   purpose and, 19

   self-evaluation of, 166

   tough messages and, 124

E

egalitarian organizations, 14–15. *See also* organizations

"Elect" step, 55, 59–61

emotions

   feedback and, 96–97, 98, 101–102, 103, 105, 106, 112, 116

   Observing Participant and, 54, 131

   tough messages and, 120, 121, 122, 124, 126, 127, 128, 131, 134, 135

empathizing, 27, 28, 32–33, 39, 40, 45, 46, 166

   feedback and, 111

   goal agreement and, 82, 83

   learning and development and, 148, 150, 152, 159

   Observing Participant and, 52, 60

   tough messages and, 135

empowerment, 87–88. *See also* personal issues

"Explore" step, 55, 58–59

expressive communication skills, 27–28, 31–32, 33–40, 43, 165. *See also* concluding; describing; questioning

   directness and, 27

   feedback and, 100

   goal agreement and, 77, 83, 84

learning and development and, 148

Observing Participant and, 60

tough messages and, 135, 137

external customers, 75

extroversion, 149, 150

F

facial expressions. *See* nonverbal communication

feedback, 5, 7, 8, 18, 19, 20, 95–118

   advance notice of, 105–106, 113

   annual performance discussions. *See* performance discussions

   anticipating, 97

   anxiety and, 96–97, 98, 101, 105, 106, 116

   asking for, 98, 106–108, 113, 115

   communication games and, 99, 111, 112

   Communication Skills and, 100, 101, 103

   competencies and, 108, 111, 113–116

   cross-purposes in delivering, 100

   customers and, 98, 99, 103, 105

   defensiveness and, 97–98, 99, 100, 103, 110

   definition of, 96

   delivery of, 105–106

   difficult situations. *See* tough messages

   directness and, 99

   emotional reactions to, 96–97, 98, 101–102, 103, 105, 106, 112, 116

   focus of, 113–116

   follow-up discussions to, 103

   forms for, 110

   functional boundaries and, 98, 99

   guidelines for, 98–116

   Guiding Principles and, 98–99, 101, 103

   as information, 101–103, 107–108, 112

   inputs, 96, 101

   intellectual reactions to, 101–102, 103

   keeping human element in, 110–113

feedback, *continued*
  learning and development and,
    114, 148
  listening template for receiving,
    109–110
  long- vs. short-term implications
    of, 113, 116
  managers and, 98, 99, 103, 105, 106,
    107–108, 110, 112
  organizational culture and, 106,
    107, 108, 110
  organizing, 101, 103–106, 109–110
  outputs, 96, 101, 111, 113–116
  performance assessment and. *See*
    performance discussions
  problems in giving/receiving,
    96–98
  as a process, 96, 101
  as a product, 96, 101
  purpose and, 92
  receivers of, 7, 96–98, 106–110,
    112–113
  respect and, 99
  responsibilities for, 98, 99, 102–103,
    106, 113
  senders of, 7, 96–98, 111–112
  shared responsibility and, 99
  sources of, 98, 110
  staff members and, 99, 105,
    107–108, 111, 112
  style, 111, 113–116
  suppliers and, 98, 99
  surveys and, 110
  team members and, 98, 103, 107,
    110, 111
  trust and, 111
forms
  effective communication and, 6
  feedback and, 110
  goal agreement and, 71
functional boundaries, 98, 99, 125. *See*
  also organizations

G

games (communication), 8, 40–46. *See*
  also names of specific games
  calling attention to, 46, 166

  Communication Skills and, 41, 43,
    45–46
  definition of, 40–41
  directness and, 43
  feedback and, 99, 111, 112
  goal agreement and, 70
  organizational culture and, 46
  performance discussions and, 111
  reasons for, 40–41
  receiver, 41, 43–46
  sender, 41–43
  social culture and, 40, 46
  tough messages and, 122, 125
gestures. *See* nonverbal
  communication
globalization, 2
goal agreement, 7, 8, 18, 19, 20, 69–94
  accountability and, 71, 78, 84
  "big picture" context, 73–77, 165
  clarity of expectations, 70, 71
  commitment to, 72–73, 88–89
  communication games and, 70
  Communication Skills and,
    82–84
  crises and, 72–73, 88, 89
  directness and, 91
  documentation of, 71
  elimination of, 91
  flexibility and, 72, 87, 88
  forms used in, 71
  guidelines for, 73–91
  Guiding Principles and, 91
  number of goals, 72
  observing and, 77
  ongoing nature of, 73, 88–91
  outputs, 71, 73, 77–86, 88, 91
  problems in reaching, 70–73
  purpose and, 91
  purpose of, 72, 73, 88, 91
  quality requirements, 71, 80–86, 87,
    91, 114
  resources and, 72, 81, 83, 84, 87, 88,
    91
  respect and, 91
  responsibilities for. *See* customers;
    managers; organizations; staff
    members; suppliers; teams

revising/renegotiating goals, 72, 87, 89, 91

roles in, 73, 77–78, 86–88. *See also* customers; managers; organizations; staff members; suppliers; teams

shared responsibility and, 91

timing and, 73

tough messages and, 125, 126

written, 91

goals. *See also* goal agreement

components of, 78–88. *See also* outputs; quality requirements

conflicts with, 88–89

Guiding Principles (of OTL), 8, 15–19, 26, 52

Communication Skills and, 26, 27

directness, 15–17, 19, 27, 43, 52, 91, 99, 124, 166

feedback and, 98–99, 101, 103

goal agreement, 91

intent and, 26

learning and development and, 145, 155

problem solving and, 165

purpose, 15, 16, 19, 27, 52, 54, 55, 58, 59, 62, 91, 92, 124

respect, 15, 16, 17, 27, 52, 91, 99, 124

shared responsibility, 15, 16, 17–19, 27, 52, 91, 99, 124

tough messages and, 124, 126, 165

H

haloing, 29

helper (role in learning and development), 147, 148, 150, 151, 152, 156, 159

hierarchical organizations, 14–15, 83–84. *See also* organizations

I

inductive thinking/learning, 149

internal customers, 75

introversion, 149, 150

It's My Duty, 41, 42

J

Junk Dealer, 42

K

knowledge (as area of learning and development), 150–151, 152, 155

Krembs, Peter, 180–181

L

learner (role in learning and development), 147, 148, 149–150, 151, 152, 156

learning and development, 5, 8, 18, 19, 20, 141–162

action plans for, 147, 154, 155

areas of, 150–151, 152, 155

attitudes/values, 150–151, 152, 155

breakdown in, 148–149

commitment to, 142, 143, 155

common problems with, 142–144

Communication Skills and, 145, 148, 155, 159

competencies and, 142, 144, 152

creativity, 150–151, 152, 155

deliberate, 142, 145–146, 150–151

development plans for, 142–143, 147, 154–157

economic values of, 159

educational experiences and, 145–146

ethic for, 145, 157–159

feedback and, 114, 148

guidelines for, 144–159

Guiding Principles and, 145, 155

helper's role in, 147, 148, 150, 151, 152, 156, 159

individuality and, 143, 145–152

induction vs. deduction, 148

knowledge, 150–151, 152, 155

learner's role in, 147, 148, 149–150, 151, 152, 156

learning styles and, 143, 149–150

nature of, 144, 145–146, 151–152

norm of, 159

observing and, 148, 159

old habits, 151, 152

opportunities for, 145, 154–157

learning and development *continued*
  outcomes of, 150–151
  outputs and, 143
  personal issues and, 151–152, 156
  personality types and, 149, 150
  planning for. *See* learning and
      development, development
      plans for
  problem solving and, 143
  process of, 144, 147–149
  purpose of, 144
  resources and, 143–144, 147, 148,
      149, 155, 156, 157
  responsibilities for, 145, 147, 148,
      149–150, 151, 152, 153
  results of, 144–145
  self-fulfilling prophecy, 153
  skills, 150–151, 152, 155
  style, 150–151, 152, 155
  support for, 152, 159
  teachers/facilitators and, 148
  unplanned, 142, 145
  vision and, 144, 147, 153–154, 155,
      156
  workplace and, 142, 143, 144, 145,
      154, 157, 159
learning ethic, 145, 157–159
learning organizations, 157, 159
learning styles, 143, 149–150
Life Saver, 42, 44, 46
listening, 27, 28, 30–32, 39–40, 45, 46,
      166
  active, 31, 53, 124, 129–130
  goal agreement and, 77, 82
  learning and development and,
      148, 150, 152
  Observing Participant and, 52, 53,
      60
  tough messages and, 126, 135, 137
listening for understanding and, 128,
      129–130. *See also* active
      listening; listening

M

managers
  communication with customers,
      84–86
  communication with staff
      members/teams, 2–3, 14, 17–18,
      28, 39
  communication with suppliers,
      83–86
  ethics of, 115
  expectations of, 70
  goal agreement and, 70, 71, 81, 82,
      83–84, 85, 87–88
  organizational structure and, 14,
      17–18
  quality requirements and, 81–82, 84
  tough messages and, 125–126, 132,
      135–136
  traditional role in communication,
      2–3
McLagan, Patricia, 179–180
McLagan Learning Systems, Inc., ix,
      181
media-based communication, 20
micromanaging, 51, 85
multidirectional feedback. *See*
      feedback, sources of; 360 degree
      feedback

N

natural teams, 87
new-age organizations, 18–19
nonverbal communication, 4, 33, 35,
      58

O

observation-importance-want
      template
  feedback and, 104–106, 109–110
  tough messages and, 127–128, 129,
      130, 134
observing, 27, 28–30, 31, 45, 46, 166
  goal agreement and, 77
  learning and development and,
      148, 159
  Observing Participant and, 52, 60
Observing Participant, 8, 51–65, 166
  Communication Skills and, 55,
      59–60, 62
  definition of, 52–53
  directness and, 52

"Elect," 55, 59–61
emotion and, 54, 131
engaging, 55–57, 61–62, 131
"Explore," 55, 58–59
practicing, 56, 61–62, 166, 167
process of. *See* "STOP" and "SEE"
   Model
purpose and, 52, 54, 55, 58, 59, 62
respect and, 52
"Sense," 55, 57–58
shared responsibility and, 52
"STOP," 55–57
timing and, 55–57
tough-message situations and, 124,
   131, 137
On-The-Level: Communication About
   Performance workshops, ix, 191
On-The-Level communication,vii–ix,
   13–23. *See also* communication;
   performance communication
applications of. *See* feedback; goal
   agreement; learning and
   development; tough messages
characteristics of, 7
Communication Skills. *See*
   Communication Skills (of OTL)
definition of, 7, 19–20
difficulty of, 7
effects of, 7–8
Guiding Principles. *See* Guiding
   Principles (of OTL)
Observing Participant. *See*
   Observing Participant
open-ended questions, 34, 35
opportunism (learning and
   development and), 145, 154–157
organizational template
feedback and, 104–106, 109–110
tough messages and, 127–128, 129,
   130, 134
organizations
charts, 87
communication games within, 46
cultures of, 6, 14–15, 46, 83–84, 87,
   106, 107, 108, 110
encouraging feedback in, 106, 107,
   108

features of, 5, 14–15, 83–84, 87
functional boundaries within, 98,
   99, 125
goals of. *See* goal agreement
hierarchical, 14–15, 83–84
information sources within, 74–75,
   76
learning, 157, 159
new-age, 18–19
planning by, 73, 74–75
priorities of, 74–75
productivity of, 17
purpose of, 75
stakeholders within, 74–75. *See also*
   customers; managers; staff
   members; suppliers; teams
outcomes (of learning and
   development), 150–151
outputs
activities versus, 78–80, 85–86
customers and, 77–78
definition of, 78
examples of, 78–81
goal agreement and, 71, 73, 77–86,
   88, 91
learning and development and, 143
teams and, 77–78

P

paraphrasing, 31, 40, 60, 152
performance communication. *See also*
   On-The-Level communication;
   performance discussions
assumptions about, 3–6
definition of, 19–20
feedback. *See* feedback
focus of, 113–116
goal agreement. *See* goal agreement
human element in, 46–47, 110–111,
   167
keys to, 165–167
learning and development. *See*
   learning and development
organizational culture. *See*
   organizations, cultures of
performance goals. *See* goal
   agreement

performance communication
continued
    personal goal for, 167
    self-esteem and, 3–4
    surprise situations, 54
    tough messages. *See* tough
        messages
performance discussions
    annual, 103
    human element in, 110–111
    ratings given in, 103, 111
    reviewing, 111, 112
    roles in, 110–111, 112
    self-evaluation and, 125
performance reviews. *See* performance
    discussions
person-to-person communication, 3,
    7, 19–20. *See also* On-The-Level
    communication
personal issues
    biases, 5, 16, 28, 31, 39, 116
    competencies, 108, 111, 113–116
    effective communication and, 5
    emotions. *See* emotions
    empowerment, 87–88
    learning and development. *See*
        learning and development
    performance, 3–4, 5–6
    self-confidence, 106
    self-esteem, 3–4, 5–6
    self-evaluation, 125, 166
    self-management, 87–88, 145
    self-talk, 52–53, 57, 59. *See also*
        Observing Participant
    style, 113–116. *See also* style (as area
        of learning and development)
    vision, 144, 147, 153–154, 155, 156
personality types, 149, 150
power and control
    abuse of, 16–17, 19
    communication and, 4, 5–6, 16–17
problem solving
    Communication Skills and, 165
    Guiding Principles and, 165
    learning and development and, 143
    tough messages and, 123, 134–137
projection, 30

purpose, 15, 16, 19
    Communication Skills and, 27
    definition of, 19
    feedback and, 92
    goal agreement and, 91
    Observing Participant and, 52, 54,
        55, 58, 59, 62
    tough messages and, 124

Q

quality requirements, 71, 80–86, 87, 91.
    See also goal agreement
    definition of, 80
    examples of, 80–81
    feedback and, 114
    resources and, 72, 81, 83, 84, 87, 88,
        91
    responsibilities for, 81–82, 84
    suppliers and, 81–82
    teams and, 81–82
questioning, 27, 33, 34–35, 40, 41, 43,
    46, 166
    feedback and, 108, 109–110
    goal agreement and, 77, 82
    learning and development and,
        159
    Observing Participant and, 52, 60
    tough messages and, 126, 135, 137
    types of questions, 34, 35, 43

R

receptive communication skills, 27,
    28–33, 39–40, 165
    feedback and, 100
    goal agreement and, 77, 83, 84
    learning and development and, 148
    Observing Participant and, 60
    tough messages and, 135
resources
    customers and, 84
    goal agreement and, 72, 75, 81, 83,
        84, 87, 88, 91
    learning and development and,
        143–144, 147, 148, 149, 155, 156,
        157
    quality requirements and, 72, 81,
        83, 84, 87, 88, 91

respect, 15, 16, 17
    Communication Skills and, 27
    goal agreement and, 91, 99
    Observing Participant and, 52
    tough messages and, 124
reviews. *See* performance discussions
role agreement, 7, 18, 19, 77–78, 86–88

S

self-confidence, 106
self-esteem, 3–4, 5–6
self-evaluation, 125, 166
self-fulfilling prophecy, 153
self-management, 87–88, 145
self-talk, 52–53, 57, 59. *See also*
        Observing Participant
"Sense" step, 55, 57–58
shared responsibility, 15, 16, 17–19
    Communication Skills and, 27
    goal agreement and, 91, 99
    Observing Participant and, 52
    tough messages and, 124
skills. *See* Communication Skills (of
        OTL communication)
skills (as area of learning and
        development), 150–151, 152,
        155
staff members
    communication among, 132
    communication with managers,
        2–3, 14, 17–18, 28, 39
    goal agreement and, 71, 74, 78, 81,
        84, 88
    organizational structure and, 14,
        17–18
    tough messages and, 125–126, 136
    traditional role in communication,
        2–3
stereotyping, 29–30
"STOP" and "SEE" Model, 54–61
"STOP" step, 55–57
style (as area of learning and
        development), 123, 131, 134,
        150–151, 152, 155
suppliers
    Communication Skills and, 77,
        82–83

communication with customers, 3,
        18, 75–77, 82–86, 98, 99, 165
    communication with managers,
        83–86
    communication with teams, 83
    educating customers, 82, 83
    goal agreement, 75–77, 81, 82–84,
        85, 86–87
    quality requirements and, 81–82
    reviewing products/services, 76
    role agreement and, 86–87

T

teachers/facilitators, 147, 148. *See also*
        helpers (role in learning and
        development)
teams
    communication among members,
        125–126, 132
    communication with managers,
        2–3, 14, 17–18, 28, 39
    communication with suppliers,
        83
    cross-functional, 87, 98
    development of, 14–15, 98
    goal agreement and, 70, 71, 74, 78,
        81, 83–84, 87, 88
    goals/expectations of, 70, 71, 72, 73,
        87
    leaders from, 87
    natural, 87
    outputs and, 77–78
    quality requirements and, 81–82
    tough messages and, 125–126
360 degree feedback, 98. *See also*
        feedback, sources of
tough messages, 5, 8, 119–140. *See also*
        feedback
    action plans and, 122, 126, 124,
        134–137
    active listening and, 124, 129–130
    anxiety and, 120, 128, 131, 135
    asking for, 126
    avoiding, 124–127, 135
    commitment to action, 122,
        134–137
    common problems, 120–124

tough messages *continued*
  communication games and, 122,
    125
  Communication Skills and, 126,
    131, 135, 137, 165
  consequences of, 122–123, 126, 129,
    134
  crises and, 121, 124–127
  customers and, 135
  defensiveness and, 127, 128, 129,
    130
  directness and, 124
  documentation of, 129
  emotions and, 120, 121, 122, 124,
    126, 127, 128, 131, 134, 135
  experience with, 123
  goals and, 125, 126
  guidelines for giving/receiving,
    124–137
  Guiding Principles and, 124, 126,
    165
  listening for understanding and,
    128, 129–130. *See also* active
    listening
  managers and, 125–126, 132,
    135–136
  objectivity of, 124, 131–134
  Observing Participant and, 124,
    131, 137
  organizational template and,
    127–128, 129, 130, 134
  personal biases and, 127, 128
  planning for, 124, 127–129, 130
  problem solving and, 123, 134–137
  purpose and, 124
  respect and, 124
  responsibilities for, 120, 121, 122,
    125, 127–128, 132, 135–137
  shared responsibility and, 124
  staff members and, 125–126, 136
  style issues, 123, 131, 134
  surprise and, 122, 123
  teams and, 125–126
  trust and, 121, 123, 127
trust. *See also* emotions
  feedback and, 111
  tough messages and, 121, 123, 127

V

value added (for customers), 71, 82, 84
values/attitudes (as area of personal
    learning and development),
    150–151, 152, 155
vision (personal), 144, 147, 153–154,
    155, 156

W

"Where Do You Stand?" feature, 20
workplace. *See also* organizations
  changes in, 2, 7–8, 88, 98
  codependency in, 18
  features of, 5
  informal contacts within, 75
  information about, 74–75
  learning and development and,
    142, 143, 144, 145, 154, 157, 159
  nature of, 2, 5, 7–8, 83–84
  power and control in. *See* power
    and control
  roles within, 2–3, 5, 9, 17–18, 28,
    74–75
  stereotypes within, 29–30
workshops (On-The-Level), ix, 191
Wounded Animal, 44
written communication, 20
  development plans and, 155
  goal agreement and, 91
  tough messages and, 127–128, 129,
    134

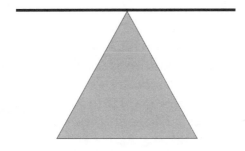

About the Authors

Patricia McLagan is chairman of McLagan International and cofounder, with her South African husband, Christo Nel, of the Democracy and Work Institute. Her major interest is helping organizations worldwide make participative processes work by developing leaders, changing management processes and systems, and providing skills and support for high levels of employee involvement and performance. As an internationally known speaker and consultant, Pat has brought innovative methods for participation and leadership to a broad range of industrial and service organizations as well as to high-technology industries and government agencies.

Pat holds a master's degree, Phi Beta Kappa, in adult education, with a special emphasis in industrial psychology and industrial relations. She is the author of many books and articles, including *The Participation Age: New Governance for Workplace and the World* (with Christo Nel), "The New Era of Leadership," "Performance Management: Can It Work?" "Systems Theory 2000," "Flexible Work Design: A Productivity Strategy for the 90s," *Helping Others Learn: Designing Programs for Adults, Getting Results Through Learning, Models for HRD Practice*, and others.

Pat is a member of the Council of Governors and past director of the American Society for Training and Development, past executive committee member for the Instructional Systems Association, and former cabinet member of the Minneapolis United Way. She has been the keynote speaker for many management, human resources, and quality conferences. She holds the highest award given by the American Society for Training and Development, the Gordon Bliss Award, and, in 1993, became the fifteenth inductee into the international HRD Hall of Fame. She is also Honorary Professor of Human Resource Development at Rand Afrikaans University in South Africa.

Peter Krembs has worked as an independent consultant since 1982. Prior to that, he was an organization development specialist for Honeywell and a partner in McLagan International.

Peter specializes in consulting to technical organizations, particularly in helping technical specialists with the transition into project leadership and management roles. He has designed and taught leadership development seminars for technical managers at several *Fortune* 500 engineering, sciences, and computer companies. He is on the faculty of General Electric's Leadership Development program, which involves teaching courses for GE businesses in Europe, Asia, India, and the United States. He is also on the faculty of the Institute for Management Studies, based in San Francisco, and teaches seminars on the transition to technical management in cities across the United States and Europe.

Peter has written several articles on the transition from technical specialist to technical manager and is author of *The Technical Manager*, a video-based training program published by Addison-

Wesley and marketed through the American Management Association. His essay "Leadership Challenges in Technical Organizations" appears in *Leadership in a New Era,* edited by John Renesch.

For more than 25 years, the name **McLagan Learning Systems (MLS)** has been synonymous with excellence in the design and delivery of innovative, results-oriented human resource programs, processes, and systems. MLS is a descendant of McLagan International, which was founded by Patricia McLagan in 1968.

MLS provides and trains clients to deliver workshops in performance management, customer-focused goal setting, team processes, and performance communication. On-The-Level: Communicating About Performance is a powerful, one-day workshop that teaches the principles and skills discussed in this book. For more information, contact McLagan Learning Systems, 715 Florida Avenue South, Suite 207, Golden Valley, Minnesota, 55426 (Phone: 612-546-5186; FAX: 612-546-5508).